Dear Mamma, Please Don't Die

Marilee Horton

Phil. 3:13

Dear Mamma, Please Don't Die

MARILEE HORTON

Thomas Nelson Publishers
Nashville

Fourth printing

Unless otherwise indicated, Scripture quotations are from the New American Standard Bible, © The Lockman Foundation 1960, 1962, 1963, 1968, 1971, 1972, 1973, 1975, and are used by permission.

Scripture quotations marked KJV are from the King James Version of the Bible.

Published in Nashville, Tennessee, by Thomas Nelson, Inc., Publishers and distributed in Canada by Lawson Falle, Ltd., Cambridge, Ontario.

Printed in the United States of America.

Library of Congress Cataloging in Publication Data

Horton, Marilee.
    Dear mamma please don't die.

    1. Horton, Marilee. 2. Christian biography—United States. 3. Multiple sclerosis—Biography. 4. Depression, Mental—Biography. I. Title.
BR1725.H664A33   248'.2   79-13455
ISBN 0-8407-5689-5

To my husband Marvin,
whose love has challenged me
to believe the abundant life
is for me too.

To my children,
Mike, Mark, Mandi, and Matthew,
who give me the grand feeling
of being needed.

CONTENTS

FOREWORD

Sometime ago at a conference where I was scheduled to speak I saw the results of a beautiful transformation caused by Jesus Christ. Listed on the program was another speaker whom I had never met. Meeting this woman was one of those unusual experiences of instant friendship and admiration. We visited briefly between meetings as time permitted and shared a couple meals together since we were staying in the same hotel. Our discussions usually centered on spiritual things and particularly on God's goodness in our lives. She spoke as a godly woman who knew Christ intimately.

The conference continued, and soon it was time for my new friend to take her part in the program. She was to give her testimony of Christ's work in her life. Judging from our brief acquaintance, I thought her story would be one of continual victory and blessing. What a surprise I had! She began to unfold her past, a story which is printed on the pages that follow. I heard how this lovely woman, who has it "all together" now, had once nearly snuffed out her life.

Today, no one would ever guess that Marilee Horton had reached such great depths of despair. How could she have come so far? I saw before my eyes a woman who had tried to destroy herself but, with God's goodness and mercy, had been saved to pick up the pieces of her broken life and start all over again.

As I listened to her story that day, I began to realize how she had become a spiritually mature woman. God had taken her through many deep waters, not to drown her but for cleansing. She had learned her spiritual lessons well.

Marilee, my friend, God has entrusted you with new opportunities for greater service—may you continue to use them for His glory. My prayer for you and the many readers of your story is that you will continue to "grow in the grace and knowledge of our Lord and Savior Jesus Christ" (2 Pet. 3:18). When any one of us takes our eyes and attention off of Christ, we begin to entertain thoughts of anxiety, apprehension, fear, and self-pity; and in time these can gradually control us. We will do well to remember this truth: "Thou wilt keep Him in perfect peace, whose mind is stayed on thee . . ." (Isa. 26:3, KJV).

Beverly LaHaye

PREFACE

It was the kind of Easter Sunday everyone hopes for. The day was bright and crisp, alive with new greenness, studded with pink and white azaleas—a day symbolic of the Resurrection. Strangely enough, it was on this meaning-filled Sunday morning that I tried to end my life.

This book is a recollection of that day and the days that followed . . . days of questions.

Why would a Christian become so despondent that death seemed the only answer? Why did I not die? Would God and my family forgive me? Would they trust me again? Would I be normal? How would my friends and fellow Christians treat me? What would I do if that strong force ever overcame me again?

The answers to these questions have brought renewed purpose to my life, and my hope is that in sharing them I will in some way help you.

Marilee Horton
May, 1979

9

Dear Mamma, Please Don't Die

ONE

Easter Sunday, 1975*

On the day I found my wife nearly dead from an overdose of sleeping pills, I had strong impressions to go home from church early. The impression was illusive at first—*Marvin, go home*—but it caused me concern. Let me say right here that I'm not given to hearing voices, nor am I very sensitive to inner suggestions; but this whole Easter Sunday morning was strange—contrary to my cool, orderly way of thinking and acting.

It wasn't strange that I was in church, since I was a minister in a children's organization. But my being in church alone on Easter was unusual. Marilee and I had been attending church as a family unit ever since the first Sunday after our wedding. However, things had changed considerably over the years; our unit had grown from two to six, and we no longer went to church just out of habit. We celebrated Sundays now because we had met the claims of Christ face to face. We had found Him to be who He said He was, and our lives had been changed. As I replayed this information in my mind, I could not conjure up the joy that was almost always present with me. For reasons I could not then understand, the impression

*I asked my husband, Marvin, to write this account of that tragic day.

13

became ocean waves hurled against my being—
Marvin, go home.

Was I uneasy just because Marilee had not come
that day? I didn't think so, because she had missed
church before. In fact, she had missed quite often
since being diagnosed as having multiple sclerosis
four years earlier. There had been many troublesome
symptoms, but mainly it was the blindness and loss
of bladder function that prevented her from going
out. Those frightening symptoms were gone now,
and, oddly enough, so was the joy that had radiated
about her during those trying days.

Now she was in constant pain with migraine
headaches, and I wondered if this was the cause of
her personality change. While trying to piece together the puzzle that was my wife, I was interrupted again with *Marvin, go home.*

I managed to squirm uncomfortably through the
service, which surprisingly ended fifteen minutes
early. I quickly rounded up three of the children,
leaving Mark to take the "bus kids" on his route, and
headed the long five miles home. Usually after
getting home I would unlock the back door, retreat,
and let the hungry children in, but not this day; I gave
in to the impression, *Marvin, something is very wrong
—you go in first.*

There are times when being the head of a household, the strong one, the rock, weighs heavy on a
man, and he envies a woman's prerogative to scream
or faint or cry. Now the message conveyed from my
eyes to my brain called for leadership, for strength
that I did not have. "Dear God, give me Your

strength," I prayed, as I leaned over my wife and brushed back the light brown hair that had fallen over her face.

She was all crumpled at the head of our long maple harvest table. The touch of my finger to her forehead, my face close to hers, confirmed the fear—something *was* wrong. She had not just dozed off; she was nearly dead. I could hardly feel the breath at her nostrils.

My sweetheart at sixteen with our dreams and love, my bride at nineteen with our future bright as the sun, the mother of our four children, my wife of nearly eighteen years lay crumpled up like a discarded green cloth. There was a chilling air of death in that room at 12:15.

There was no time for figuring things out. The children were stunned and frightened, and my barking out orders seemed a welcome relief. Michael, seventeen, blond, sensitive, and most like his mother, was sent to call an ambulance. Mandi, eleven and untouched as yet by any sadness, was crying as she took Matthew, five, into the living room. He kept asking, "Has Mamma fainted?"

Once alone in the kitchen with that bent form, I knew I had to do something. She had always responded to my touch, either warmly and drawing near or coolly and pulling away, but now there was no response; she was just a shriveled, green form—like someone from some horror movie. One eye would not close completely and stared blankly. I wondered, even in this macabre situation, if she was watching to see if I performed satisfactorily.

Why had she done it? Was she disappointed because none of us, including her, could live up to her perfectionist standards?

In the next few days I was to ask "why" hundreds of times. Why *Marvin, go home?* Why not a flat tire? Why not a delay? Why not the usual time for the sermon?

During those first confused moments which seemed like an eternity, I stood there—loving her, hating her; wishing she were busy as usual cooking lunch; wishing I had never met such a complex person; hoping she were already dead, then begging God to let her live. How could so many contradictory thoughts flit in and out of one mind so rapidly?

Unable to lift her, I watched her slip heavily from my arms to the black and white tiled floor. Vain attempts to revive her were abandoned. Was the face-slapping more than an attempt to bring life to that morbid face? Could there be anger welling up inside of me? Water poured on her face only formed ugly pools on each side of her head in which I could see reflections of myself—Marvin Horton, the optimist, the man who had it all together. Who had botched this up?

I had always known what to do in most situations, but now I drew a blank. "God, You promised to deliver us if we called upon You in the day of trouble, and this is it," I prayed. Suddenly I knew what had happened. Marilee had not fainted; she had tried to end her life at the age of thirty-six.

Rushing back from the phone where I was able, miraculously, to reach her doctor on the first call to the hospital, I dashed into the bathroom by our bedroom and found the empty bottle that had contained sleeping pills.

Within minutes I heard the sound that always before had been a rude, unwelcomed scream blaring its grim news to anyone within hearing distance. I breathed my first sigh of relief. It was to be my last for a long time. I joined the children in a gasp when the rescue squad member, in a matter-of-fact tone, said, "I can get no pulse or respiration." The team that efficiently placed the resuscitator tube in her throat and pounded so professionally on her chest had been trained only days earlier by the head nurse of the hospital emergency room, which soon received what was left of my wife. This was their first experience.

Somehow, the woman I loved, a Christian known and loved for her testimony of how Jesus Christ had given meaning to her life, had tried to slip quietly out of our lives. Had Christ been unable to meet her need? Deep within I knew that the matter was in God's hands and that this suicide attempt could never be kept quiet. I really believed Romans 8:28: "And we know that all things work together for good to them that love God, to them who are the called according to his purpose" (KJV).

I believed that if she died I would be given the grace to share something good from her death. That today Marilee is living and willing to share that painful portion of her life brings meaning to what was a time of puzzling confusion.

TWO

Monday— Intensive Care

My first waking recollections were not very concrete—just colors and sounds.

Even before the enormous struggle of opening my eyes, I heard an unfamiliar beeping and a "suction-swoosh" sound. I don't know how long I lay there trying to figure out what I was hearing.

I seemed to be floating in space. The only weight I felt was my eyelids. Just opening them was such a chore that I gave up many times before I actually did it; and when I did open them, it was just long enough to see a white ceiling and a large stainless steel circular contraption with plastic bags of fluids hanging on it.

I don't know if moments or hours passed before I had the strength to push open my eyelids again. A blurred white form bent over me and gently touched something near my mouth or in it. Out of the corner of my eye I saw figures, large and small in shades of blue, green, and yellow.

Trying to stay awake or speak was futile. Everything went black again. Then, once more, my eyes and my mind weakly made contact with both the unknown and the known.

There were hushed voices saying, "Honey . . . Mamma . . . wake up." I could barely feel my hands being rubbed. The stainless steel circle overhead confused me. It seemed to be going around, but the tubes that hung down stayed in a fixed position. There were tubes in both arms. I felt a slight pressure just under my nose from the tube going in my right nostril, and there was something in my throat. Out of the corners of my eyes I could see odd machines and I wanted to inquire, but the sleep that I had bought was sweet and I sank back into the abyss.

Each time I woke I was more aware. The hushed voices were those of my husband, Marvin, and our two older sons, Mike and Mark. Each time I opened my eyes I noticed Mike's hand on mine. There was a "hurt puppy" look in his eyes.

All the tubes and the noisy machines were somehow connected to my weightless body. I could not feel any pain; neither was I capable of emotion.

Little by little I became more alert for the few moments that I was conscious before slipping back into black-purple oblivion. I began trying to figure things out. The two white patches on my chest had wires running to what I knew to be a heart monitor; its beeping sound was assuring those who cared that my heart was beating properly. I was not afraid of the cold and ugly machines; they seemed to be my friends in an all new, sterile world.

More than a few minutes passed between my moments of consciousness. The children had changed clothes. Funny that I should have noticed that while I was suspended in some kind of twilight zone.

All of this momentary waking took place in the early morning hours on Monday. At 8:40 Monday morning I was jolted awake by a strong force that I now know was the Lord. I was unusually alert for someone so near death. Somehow through the reflection in the glass window between me and the nurses' station I could see a clock. In the midst of not knowing anything, I suddenly knew what day and time it was and that I had to drive kindergarten carpool. I had no idea of the importance of what was going on in my head—the fact that I was thinking clearly.

I had to let my family know of my carpool responsibility—but how? Those unemotional, nonunderstanding machines that I was married to were hindering me. I weakly motioned for my husband to come close and I tried to talk. I was frustrated to find out that I couldn't speak with the tube in my throat.

At this very moment they moved close and a nurse unscrewed the tube at my mouth, leaving the inner one inserted. They were trying to get me to breathe on my own, but with people watching me and the added frustration of not being able to speak, I felt as if I were suffocating. The figures seemed about twice my size; I was afraid, and panic set in. They reconnected the tube and I relaxed.

Time was running out; I had to tell them about the carpool! Sensing my desperation in trying to communicate, Marvin held up a small chalkboard and placed a piece of chalk in my hand. Although it took great effort, I could raise my hand about three inches, but I couldn't keep it elevated. Slumber hit again, but not without a fight. Sleep was no longer sweet; I wanted to be awake. I did not realize what was really going on—God was giving my frightened, tired family a precious and clear sign that their fears about the near certain brain damage were unnecessary.

When I woke again it was 9:00 A.M. I began to move my hands in a driving motion with everyone in the room joining in as if we were playing charades:

"You want me to drive somewhere?"

NO! I shook my tube-infested head as violently as I could.

Again I tried steering the car, but this time I added a final clue, and it was a stroke of God's genius. I pointed to myself and the light dawned on them.

"You have kindergarten carpool?"

Just before sinking into about two more days of silence, I saw my doctor, a fine Christian and a friend, shoot a relieved look to my family.

After a couple of days my waking periods lengthened and my awareness grew keener. For instance, I knew that the thing going up and down with regularity was a resuscitator. The tube in my nose was performing its grim task of reaping with all its might the residue of forty sleeping pills that I had sown into my stomach. I was in the intensive care unit (ICU) and people were coming to the door, praying, and leaving. I could hear the nurse say, "Mr. Horton, you must get these people out of here." They were not as strict for some reason as they usually are.

The Father knew that Marvin and the children needed not only the knowledge that people were praying but also the supportive evidence of a touch and a tear.

At one point I heard the nurse say, "Mr. Horton, there have been over seventy people in this ICU, and while they mean well, they are congesting a very important area—send them to the chapel to pray."

Many friends and ministers stayed through the night. Yet foreign to my introspective nature, I was not responding in an emotional way to what I had done or what was being done around me.

The only thing I felt was fear each time they unscrewed the resuscitator tube at my mouth. Of course, I remember most clearly the last time the nurse did that. She encouraged me much as a coach encourages his team: "You can do it; breathe for me, baby, breathe."

A great shout rang in the hall when I took a deep, natural breath. The question as to how long I should be kept alive by artificial means had been answered. "Hallelujah" and "Praise the Lord" echoed up and down the corridors. Those who had prayed and fasted through the nights and days had not done so in vain.

Yes, I was breathing, and with that very first breath came the responsibilities of life. No longer did I succumb to deep sleep every few moments. Realities were slapping me hard in the face again. Questions were forming in my mind and heart. Sorrow over what I had done was mixed with an unexpected joy over being given another chance. The state of being unemotional had not been normal for me; the hot tears gathering in the corners of my eyes were most welcome.

That Wednesday I was wheeled—bed, bottles, and wires—down the hall to a regular hospital room. It was not in a psycho ward, nor a criminals' ward, but in a typical recovery ward, just a regular room with a window. My heart beat faster at the sight of the bright greens and blues of the great outdoors. I could not understand my own feelings.

Just a few days earlier life had been so bleak, so full of pain and self-rejection that I had found it impossible to go on. Now I was swelling up inside with joy at being alive. That was confusing.

I didn't even mind still being attached to some of my friends from ICU: catheter, IV, heart monitor. The doctors' whisperings about transferring me to a hospital with dialysis equipment did not disturb me.

When the decision was made that I was not strong enough for transfer, my Christian urologist trusted my damaged kidneys to the Great Physician. Before my first day in a regular room was over, thanksgiving prayers were offered when I was able, with the help of my husband on one side and my best friend on the other, to make the trip to the bathroom, empty my bladder, and get back into bed before the nurse could put in a new catheter. The heart monitor relationship was also severed that day.

I was in familiar surroundings. I had spent considerable time here and in the university hospital in Birmingham for diagnostic tests, which had revealed multiple sclerosis, and more recently for neurological tests, which had revealed that there was no physiological cause for the weeks of agonizing headache pain.

Shortly after settling me in my room, a nurse's aide brought in my mint green gown that had been cut at the shoulders when the ambulance driver handed my all but dead body to the hospital staff. Under that was my dark green robe. Under the sleeve of that robe was a tiny, torn piece of paper from a yellow legal pad; it looked only too familiar. Tears welled up and stung my eyes as I opened the little note and read: "Dear Mamma, please don't die. Love, Mandi."

The tears were spilling down my cheeks and falling in profusion onto the little yellow note, smudging the words; and I cried out, "Dear God, what have I done to her, to everyone, and why?" I clutched to my heart the little note written in the frantic horror and haste of what she must have witnessed that day. My stomach ached as I wondered, "What will that memory do to her?" That was something I would have to live with.

Yes, I would live.

God thought that note important enough to allow Mandi to run and place it on me while I was being wheeled into the ambulance. The nurses found it and thought it important enough to keep with my other belongings. Yes, it was important. That message from my eleven-year-old daughter was enough to give me the beginnings of courage, the foothold of a better self-image, and enough love to cement together the fragments of my broken life. I would live. That little girl deserved a Mamma and even a poor, ill Mamma was better than none at all.

"Dear God, where are You?" I cried.

With sweet assurance to my weeping heart, the Word of God came to me: "I'm here, my child, I never left you. I will *never* leave you nor forsake you."

"Dear Father, I'm sorry. Can You forgive this horrible sin against You? How could someone who loved You so much fail so miserably?" Again, God spoke through His Word hidden in my heart. "I am faithful and just to forgive your sins and to cleanse you from all unrighteousness" (see 1 John 1:9).

My emotions were active again, and I felt a tempest going on inside of me; but I clung to the Rock that is higher than I. A great forgiveness rolled over my being, and the peace that had characterized my life in Christ came back. It was a blessed gift from God.

No Mandi, Mamma won't die. Just for you. I love you too.

THREE

The Source

I call it the "ripple principle." Our actions affect those around us in greater or lesser degrees, much like a stone thrown into a pond affects the water. It is especially sad in my case because of the sensitive children involved. I know that each of my children carries the weight at times of unwarranted blame and guilt for my decision to quit living. For that I will forever be genuinely sorry.

I am not even aware of just what psychological damage this act has done to my children, but I know the nagging burden of guilt has taken its toll. Regardless of the talks to expiate this burden, it remains.

My first knowledge that I had in fact thrown a giant boulder into the pond and set in action the "ripple principle" came on Tuesday, while I was still in intensive care.

I assume I had made some promising responses to the gentle, persistent urgings to wake up. Everything was like an old black and white film, and the grayness hovered over the sterile whiteness like a city smog. Perhaps it was just that time of day, either before the sun rises or after the sun sets (they call it twilight, but to me that word sounds too pretty); I didn't really have any way of knowing.

The clock through the glass cubicle said 6:10, and it could have been A.M. or P.M. (I now know it

27

was A.M.) I had very few feelings at that time, but what I felt fit the mood—gray and clammy. The various forms in the room moved around and whispered as if at a funeral.

Our sons, seventeen and fifteen, were on either side of the bed, each with their hands holding and rubbing one of mine saying, "Mamma, please wake up . . . open your eyes." I had tried before, but now I would try harder, just for them. It was with supreme effort that I stretched my eyelids open.

I was puzzled and I must have looked it. Everything seemed to move around me like a circular film, and I was the one and only spectator. Suspended in space, attached by foreign connections, almost inhuman, I could relate to no one else.

They made their move as if they had been waiting for a sign to get absolution from some weighty sin, or healing from some dread disease. Both fell across me simultaneously, and plaintively, repeatedly sobbed, "We're sorry; we're sorry."

My mind rose to the occasion in its normal maternal fashion, but "Oh dear God, why won't my arms move, my mouth? Why do I just lie here like a great Buddha, accepting the sacrifice of children?"

I prayed, "Precious Father, You must comfort them, if they are to be comforted at all."

Since my brain was the only active member of my body, I began doing mental gymnastics, jumping from the pitiful sight of two tall, healthy boys tumbled in a heavy, crushed heap on my chest. They were actually clinging to each other, squeezing me in the middle. Why did they seem so sad and pitiful?

I mentally pole-vaulted to my most recent

recollection—back two days to Easter Sunday morning. I remembered that I had not slept well the night before, in spite of taking several sleeping pills. I had often wondered if I were addicted to sleeping pills, because I was taking more and more and they were doing less and less. Of course, I would have denied any such talk.

I remembered that I had rather perfunctorily made my morning rounds on that morning, first upstairs and through the large game room into Mike's room.

He always needed an extra half hour of uninterrupted bathroom privileges. Getting ready was a ritual with him. He showered so long that we needed a few minutes to let the water heat up again before anyone else could bathe. The tons of towels he used had to be hauled out and the steam wiped off the mirror when he finished.

The most elaborate production was the hair. Before hand blowers became available, he would lie flat on his back with his head hanging over the blower of the floor furnace.

The very last thing he did was to spread a clean towel over his lap, take his contact case, squirt fluid on the lenses, and then plop them into his eyes. Then I knew he was on his way, and we might not be late for church after all.

He was very meticulous but an absolute "bear" in the morning. All I ever said as I pulled the three covers and two pillows off his face was, "Last call, you had better get up. . . . Okay, I am going to get your Dad."

That particular morning, however, I felt like a flesh-colored robot. If Mike snarled at me I didn't notice; for some reason it didn't matter. It was as if the responsibility for his morning manners was not mine anymore. I was just fulfilling a role.

Usually after Mike was up for about an hour, he would begin singing, and all the anger and frustration I felt would melt in the sunshine of the love that glued our relationship together. As I heard that tenor voice that was great at seventeen, which had already won him an important scholarship, I knew one day he would be grand. I knew I would laugh then at his idiosyncrasies. But not that morning. He could have sung the entire "Hallelujah Chorus," solo and a cappella, and I would have remained unmoved.

I had expected too much of my family and especially of myself. My goals for us were so high that they were virtually unattainable. The more we failed to reach my perfect standards, the more I turned in on myself in anger. I blamed myself for failing to establish the "perfect, happy, Christian family."

As I look back now, four years later, I see that most of the normal unpleasantries that go with raising several children really do pass. As I look at the three older children, I see responsible, productive, well-adjusted young adults. Somehow the bickering, selfishness, and rivalry are locked away in mental trunks labeled "Childhood Foolishness."

It all seems so petty now. Yet, those years that should have been fun were marred by dark clouds that spelled out *failure*. I wanted to see the end result before the end. I should have remembered that infants don't behave as toddlers, and adolescents don't act in a responsible, respectable adult manner before their time.

I wish someone had said to me, "Hey, you expect

too much. Give them a few more years and you will be surprised by the good job you have done." And I am.

Not being in a rational frame of mind, however, I crept back down the stairs, walked through the high-ceilinged, celery-colored living room, which before had always brought me a sense of calm and joy, down the hall, and into my bedroom. I deposited myself into a gold corduroy reading chair by the fireplace, whereupon I read my daily three chapters from the Bible.

For about the third straight week I was unmoved by God's written Word. Before this period God's Word had always met a very personal need in my life.

I decided to forego my daily devotional reading from *Streams in the Desert*, by Mrs. Charles Cowman, gloomily deciding that nothing could help me.

That was unfortunate because on that day, March 30, I would have read about a solemn warning to those who walk in temporary darkness and yet who try to help themselves out into the light. It told about the temptation we have when our way is gloomy to find a way out without trusting in the Lord. We accept the conclusions of our own reason and are tempted to accept a way of deliverance that would not be the Lord's way. It went on to say that premature deliverance may frustrate God's work of grace.

Had I read it, maybe I would have realized that what was about to happen to me was not God's way out. It might have given me the courage and fortitude needed to wait on God's deliverance.

I shall now always remember that we cannot fight

the forces of darkness alone but that we need God's written Word as well as testimonies and encouragement from His children who have walked this path before.

God could have used His Word to say to me, "Dear child, I know it is dark, but I will hold your hand if you will just hold on." But instead I listened to my enemy, the spirit of heaviness. I had opened a door labeled "self-pity" and had bid him enter and rest a while in the cool, dark chamber of my mind. I had made him welcome and had taken his advice and pity as I would have from an old friend. I am so ashamed when I think of "the Friend that sticketh closer than a brother" and how I grieved and quenched His Spirit.

I heard Mike thump down the hall, so back up the stairs I went with a heavy sigh of resignation, bent over like an old charwoman. Every step was a mountain. I bent to wake Mark. He was sleeping in his usual position, flat on his back, straight as an arrow. He was as dark as Mike was light, a striking, handsome boy with an equally handsome disposition . . . that was, until his temper flared. Marvin said that it was the Cherokee Indian inherited from his side of the family that made Mark rage so when things didn't go his way. He could charm the socks off of you if he wanted to though.

All I had to do was touch his lean, hard shoulder and he fairly shot out of bed and ran down the stairs. "So much like his dad," I thought as I heard the shower running again. So unlike his older brother. They had rather enjoyed a sublime case of sibling rivalry from the moment a blond nineteen-month-old "king bee" had to move over for a brown-haired "brodder." They fought tooth and toenail down through the years. They seemed to actually hate each other. I turned that in on myself as another failure: "Something must be wrong with me." When they were tiny they would count who had one more Cheerio than the other. Or one would scream in real horror, "Mom, he's looking at me again!" The other would gasp in unbelief, "Mom, he touched me; *gross*, he's dirty!"

As teen-agers they were more sophisticated, but the venom was there. They were totally unalike and they intended to rub it in. Often they would get me involved in a silly squabble that really had no fair solution, and I would always be accused of favoring one or the other. The good student called the other stupid, while the good athlete called the other a sissy. It all hurt the whole family, and I didn't know the answer; I just tried to keep them separated.

Eventually, they would push me to the limit during their battles, and I would push the button on my mental tape recorder and the same speech would hatefully spew out: "You are determined to drive me crazy; that is your whole purpose and goal in life. I can never have a moment's peace . . . have mercy on me." But the one that stung the most was, "The Lord must be real proud of you two. We might as well give up trying to live a Christian life. We could do it if it weren't for you."

I would scream in the sheer frustration of knowing that I was not reacting to pressure and stress in the right way. So, I would blame them for the whole mess. I always felt like a big heel after my outburst, but I knew that just as I couldn't remove the holes in the wall when I jerked the nails out, so I couldn't repair the little nail holes I put in their lives. When I thought of the weight of that millstone, I was sick to my stomach. And I internalized one more guilt trip.

Another problem that plagued me constantly was the fact that Mike was musical and not at all athletic. In our culture where a ball is god, whether it be small and fuzzy, small and hard, or large and enroute to a basket or oval, those who don't join the cult are looked upon with suspicion. Well, try as we did from the time Mike was five years old, he would not pay homage to that god. At the age of five he didn't realize the severity of the social punishment for refusing to bow at such shrines. Whereas we Americans have adored athletes and "jocks," those not into sports are sometimes called "strange" and "queer." Jokes are made of them, and even teachers make remarks that cut to the core.

The saddest thing was that, in our desire to have Mike accepted by the game-worshiping culture, we refused to accept him for a long time for what God had made him to be. The cracks and digs made by his own brother labeled him "sissy" and hurt the very center of his being.

In trying to make up for the hurt caused by Mark and unintentionally by his father, I overcompensated. I let him get by with more. I covered for and sided with him, and many times he took advantage of this; then Mark was hurt.

I still don't know the easy way out of this kind of situation, but I do know that God creates us with different and divinely bestowed gifts. Somehow we must provide the healthy space for a child to find his niche. Time has solved this problem for us. Mike is in graduate school, having won literally thousands of dollars in scholarships because of his fine tenor voice. He has spent his summers singing with an opera company and plans a career in the opera. He has had this goal since he was about sixteen and has hung onto it and not veered off the course. He knew what he wanted and he is going after it, often with very little help.

I might add that we went as a family to Birmingham Southern College during Mike's junior year for his recital, and it was the first recital Mark had attended. When he realized the incredibly hard work that went into a recital in four languages, a recital that was very nearly perfect, he openly wept and embraced his brother. Years of hostility melted away.

Mark has been an easy child to raise because he isn't very temperamental and he isn't difficult to please. He makes friends rapidly and finds joy in doing many things. He is now studying for the ministry, and we couldn't be prouder of him. Somehow we feel that even the hard years of misunderstanding and hurt have been years of training for the futures of these two fine young men that I am proud to call my sons.

But on that Easter Sunday morning these realities were not even in the realm of future hope. There was a skirmish in the kitchen, but I don't remember what it was over. I had given Matthew, five, and Mandi, eleven, their Easter baskets, had helped them put on their new Easter finery, and had given them breakfast. All the while, I was trying to goad myself into at least making a pretense of joy over the most important Christian holiday.

I had begun to believe that my lips couldn't smile ever again.

When the fight occurred, I said angrily, "You can all just go without me. I am too tired to fight it anymore." With all the self-pity I could muster, I crept to my bed in defeat.

Before leaving for church, Marvin sat down beside me on our old canopy bed and tenderly kissed my hand saying, "What is wrong, Honey?"

"I'm just tired," I murmured, pulling away. "I think I'll take a sleeping pill and see if I can get some sleep for a couple of hours."

Mike was the last to come in and see me, and his green eyes were misty. He said he knew I was upset over his relationship with Mark, which he knew was not pleasing to the Lord. He said he planned to meet Mark at the altar in church that morning and get it settled. Keeping my eyes cruelly closed, I acted as if I neither believed him nor cared.

Mark had been picked up a few moments earlier by the bus that he worked on for the church's bus ministry. So it was four of them who climbed into our blue Buick station wagon while I climbed deeper and deeper into my blue pit from which chances of rescue were slim and not at all invited.

Up until this point, I had not committed myself to a plan. I really intended to take one sleeping pill when I entered the bathroom, but just at that moment the enemy of my soul struck like a snake. My defenses were down because I had been listening to his consolations of pity, not realizing that this was a war tactic pulling me away from my protective cover. I looked in the mirror at a beaten woman with dark circles under green, puzzled eyes and cried out, "Dear God, what went wrong?"

Then I passively yielded to an inner voice so strong that I physically felt the force of his command: "Take them all, you are no good—no good as a wife, as a mother, and most of all, no good to God. He has stamped FAILURE over your name."

My heart raced. I took the large red container that had been entrusted to me by physicians who really wanted to relieve me of pain. I know I had shown no signs of despair or I couldn't have gotten so many pills at one time. I took the bottle to my bed and dumped the precious cargo onto the white sheet. They were long and green and shimmered in the streaked sunlight like a pile of emeralds.

I counted them. "Forty. That should be sufficient to bring my family peace."

Then I resisted the dark force, put one pill into my mouth, and pushed the thirty-nine others back into the bottle. I returned to the bathroom to put the bottle up where the serpent was waiting to strike again, "Go ahead Mrs. FAILURE, take them all." Then he said, "Your family has been saddled with an invalid too long. Let them get on with living. Show them you love them by getting out of their way."

That was the last straw. One by one, I swallowed thirty-nine more of the smooth, green promisers of relief.

I bathed and slipped into a pair of lace panties that were still new. They had been too small when I received them amid giggles at my birthday party the previous August. I thought, "Strange how they now fit with room left over." I also donned a pale green gown given by some dear friends at the same party.

If I had been thinking clearly, I would have seen that everything I wore that morning was a gift of love. I would have remembered a friend's house on the eighth of August crowded with laughing people who enjoyed surprising me with mountains of gifts. I chose to listen to the master of deceit say, "No one cares about you; you are alone." And I believed his lie.

I was not judging the time very well, but then how could I? I had never tried to kill myself before. I was already beginning to feel intoxicated and euphoric as I quickly slipped a ham and sweet potatoes in the oven. Satan convinced me that a nice dinner would make up for my trouble to my family . . . sort of an added touch of class. As I set the long, maple harvest table, I began to have trouble focusing and I knew my time had come.

I grabbed a yellow legal pad and began to first write a note to the children. They must know that it wasn't their problems that had brought me to this point—I had just used that against them. I knew almost every family had similar problems . . . I had to let them know they were not to blame, that I was just copping out so they could have a better life. . . . I managed to struggle through the word "Dear," but try as I might, I couldn't keep my hand from scratching across the page as I laid my head down and entered a land of profound, black unconsciousness.

Five miles north of the house, Easter rejoicing was taking place as it was in the hearts of millions of

Christians everywhere. Pastel-clad children of God were celebrating the Resurrection in song. At the close of the service, our two sons would respond to an invitation. Mike and Mark would meet at the altar to confess their animosity, vow to accept and love each other, and sign a peace treaty—one that they could hardly wait to come home and share with a mother who was no longer waiting. I am sorry I was not able to receive that message then, but what days of sunshine and songs could not bring about, days of grim, agonizing grief did.

Now come back with me to the hospital room where my waiting sons were still hugging me. I prayed, "Heavenly Father, kind Shepherd of these tender boys, I can see that I was tricked. These boys do need a mother. So I don't have all the answers and I am not patient or perfect, but I could iron that old wrinkled shirt Mark is wearing. Lord, if you will give me another chance I want to try again. Just let me assure them that no matter how I fail, they are not responsible."

A couple of days later when my arms could hug again, Mark brought me a small, sweet, green plant and a card telling me that he loved me and that I was the best mother in the world. That plant has grown a lot, and I think I have grown with it. Every time I give it a drink I say, "Little plant, you are the best little plant in the whole world because you remind me that to four children, whose names begin with M, I am the best mother in the whole world." You know, I am beginning to believe that.

I hope that in squeezing my children tightly and

whispering in their ears "You are the best children," I have been able to erase every cobweb of doubt and guilt. I don't know yet for sure. But I am beginning to examine my faulty system of checks and balances, seeing how different it is from God's.

He says, "Of course, you don't deserve My love, but by My grace I want to give it to you."

No matter what my children do to me or me to them, as a parent I can't stop loving them. I have also seen that they want to forgive me and that they won't stop loving me, either. What advice would I give squabbling families? "Be kind to one another, tenderhearted, forgiving each other . . ." (Eph. 4:32).

If you are the son or daughter of a suicide victim, please, please understand that no matter what you did, you are not the source of the tragedy. In our family relationships we do wound each other, but the wounds are not mortal. Satan is the foe. If he has deceived your parent into giving up on life, the next step in his plan is to ruin your life with guilt. If you are a Christian you need not lose this battle. Philippians 3:13, 14 provide your escape:

> Brethren, I do not regard myself as having laid hold of it yet; but one thing I do: *forgetting* what lies behind and *reaching forward* to what lies ahead, I press on toward the goal for the prize of the upward call of God in Christ Jesus (italics mine).

You can turn your back on the past and say, "I will forever be sorry that my parent died in that way, but that is past and no matter what I do, I cannot change that. I can, however, change *me* by the power of

Christ." Then turn the page on your calendar and start a new day with a prayer: "Father, take away any guilt that I might be bearing and help me to live my life to its fullest potential." Thank your heavenly Father, and reach out. Someday you will understand better the dark things of this life.

If you are not a Christian, you will not find relief outside the fold of Jesus Christ. I would urge you to admit to God that you are a sinner (see Rom. 3:23), acknowledge His love (see John 3:16), thank Him (Jesus) for dying on the cross for you and for having the power to come alive again, receive Him as your Savior, and be clean (see John 1:12). The same power that raised Him from the dead can change your life and mine.

FOUR

Till They Have Fallen

It was Friday, the fourth of April. Just five days had passed since my curious Easter morning actions. I had a wonderful peace in my heart, which I had received the moment I confessed to God that what I had done was a sin against Him.

I was humming softly as I brushed back my short, damp hair. I had taken a soothing, warm shower and put on the expensive oriental print pajamas Marvin had brought me the day before. The sheets were cool and crisp like the April morning. As I looked out my fourth-floor window I could see colors bursting through the fresh green. Pink and white azaleas, yellow daffodils, dogwoods, and red tulips studded the ground like so many jewels. I almost wished I had a canvas and my oil paints. "Oh, yes, that is another wonderful thing I can do when I take up my life again," I mused.

It was 9:00 in the morning. As I climbed into bed at a time of day when I should have been driving kindergarten carpool and then catching up on washing for six busy people and cleaning a thirteen-room house, I thought again about my "problem." The problem was that I had not been coping too well with life in general. I wondered just what would be done with me. I didn't know anyone who had attempted to commit suicide and failed, so I didn't know the procedure. I had seen one TV show where they put the poor, deranged person in a jail cell and another one where the person was locked in a psycho ward with people who rocked back and forth all day crying. Those dreary thoughts removed the joy the flowers had given, and I realized there was still an emotional tug of war going on inside of me. "Maybe I do need to be put away," I thought with a shudder.

I was really feeling nearly normal again. It was as if the drug overdose was like a shock treatment. Just the sound of "drug overdose" made me feel ashamed. The depression was gone, and I couldn't even comprehend how I could have done such a thing. It was as if I had read about someone else's doing it.

Other than being too thin, I looked well enough. Too thin was a problem I didn't often have. I kind of enjoyed walking down the hall and weighing myself and thinking of the things I could eat to regain the twenty pounds I had lost. That, too, posed a big problem since everything I put into my mouth would swell and become tasteless and fuzzy like cotton balls. I sent everything back, much to the dismay of the nurses and aides who would shake their heads and say, "We must eat all our dinner."

Loss of appetite is a danger signal that depression has worsened, and the physician finally told me that until I began to get the food assimilation process in motion again I might as well kiss my home goodbye. I began swallowing everything like it was medicine because I really did want to get well. I have always enjoyed cooking and eating so much that it was hard to imagine my being in that predicament.

About 10:00 Marvin brought the two older boys up to see me. It seemed so unnatural for them to be visiting me so formally. We tried to be light-hearted and chatty, and I smiled at myself as I thought, "It will be good to see them take a few verbal swipes at each other; then I will know we are back to normal."

At 10:30 the aide came into the room with my mail. There were five cards, but for my eyes there was only one. Marvin was teasing the young black aide, but my heart had nearly stopped. I was holding an envelope with my name written by a hand that could belong only to my father. As I paused too long on that long, slim envelope, Mark cried, "It's from Grandpa —open it, Mom!"

They could never have comprehended what was going on in my heart and mind. How could they have known that I had never, to my knowledge, had a card or letter from my daddy? I knew that if I were that shaken by seeing my name in his handwriting, I was surely emotionally unprepared to open it.

Amid 'Oh, Moms," I just propped it up against my glass of newly crushed ice and looked at it. . . . "Marilee Horton . . ."

As far back as I could remember, I had desperately wanted to know just what my dad thought and felt about me. I had worked very hard trying to prove that I was someone he could be proud of. "Oh Dear God," I thought, "after all these years of not know- ing if I had quite made the grade, now, after a splashy fall, he writes." If my state had not been so critical, it would have been funny.

Tears were standing on the precipice of my lower lashes, ready to jump. I commanded them to stay. I would not cry, not then. Looking down, I began to rub the swelling around a large hole made by one of the IV tubes that had run into my right arm. I swallowed hard and continued to look down until I became composed.

Somehow I managed to get through the long forty-five minutes until my family left the room. Once alone, I rather timidly picked at the flap of the white envelope. Suddenly, all the things I wished I had had the courage to tell Daddy flooded through my mind: "I admire you so and want to be like you." He was so quiet, and somehow I was afraid to talk to him. I don't know why.

He wasn't a frightening man but a gentle one. Oh sure, he had a pretty hot temper, but generally he was very quiet. He was a good, decent, moral man. I could never understand my craving for his approval, nor did I understand how I wanted him to show it. It never dawned on me that his silence might be approval.

I do remember Mom's asking him why he never told her the meals she prepared were good (and they were). He replied, "If they weren't good, I wouldn't eat them." I guess I should have gotten a clue from that. In his quiet strength he seemed so perfect, so disciplined—all the things I was not. In the eight years I had been a Christian I especially wanted to show him the peace and joy that Christ had given me. Boy, what a mess I had made of things. How could I ever show him that Christ had not let me down but I had let Him down?

The envelope was open and I was trembling so hard it was difficult to get the card out.

"Stupid, take it out!" I sternly thought. "The last thing he would do is pick a time like this to tell you what a disappointment you are. The least thing it could say is 'Love, Dad.' " I did so long for more of a message than that, and I wasn't disappointed.

My daddy is a shy, sensitive man and out of respect for those qualities I won't embarrass him by printing every word. I know that for my family a book of this nature is embarrassment enough. But because lack of communication has caused so many family members to think they are unloved, I feel compelled to share this to encourage those of you in that category to give each other the benefit of the doubt. Believe you are loved.

The card began, "Dear Mike." That was an endearing nickname that he called me until I married. I both loved and hated it. I went through a period when I believed he was disappointed that I was a girl. I tried to play ball but was a classic sports washout. But that day I knew my nickname was one way he had of telling me I was special and loved.

The note said something like, "I am not very articulate, but you must know you are one of my favorite loved ones." That was like a healing balm. He urged me not to worry about what people thought or said about what I had done, "Remember the old Indian proverb about not judging a person until you have fallen out of the same tree."

That was all I needed. Tears, burning, streaming down my face, washed away all doubt about my standing with my earthly father. I stood accepted just as I was with my heavenly Father—undeserving but accepted. The walls of my own making came tumbling down. He understood, he cared; and ''he loves me,'' I said aloud.

The following week when Mom and Dad came to the hospital to see me, Mom told me of the afternoon that Dad labored over that message. He wrote and rewrote, had Mom read it, then wrote it again.

Words don't flow easily for him, or cheaply. I was sorry for what those words cost, but I treasured them. And I loved him more than ever, and the respect I felt for him was more than special. I guess that was why I wanted his approval—if he could approve, then all the world surely would. I had fallen, but like the heavenly Father, Daddy was willing to pick me up like a fragile baby bird and protect me from the winds of anyone else's disapproval.

How do these obstructions get in the way, making a daughter think she is unacceptable and unloved when in fact just the opposite is true? Is that too the work of the enemy of our soul who loves to sow discord among families? I think it is. If the teller of lies can convince us that our earthly fathers don't love us, it is then very easy for us to disbelieve God's love. Isn't our view of our father often carried over to our view of God?

I certainly don't have all the answers concerning the fragile elements of human relationships, but one important thing I have learned is that we are all of different temperaments, and what is easy for me to express may be painfully difficult for another. The very qualities that I love in my calm, undemonstrative dad usually tie in with the qualities that I do not understand. For every temperament strength there is a temperament weakness to correspond.

It happens all the time in a marriage. You fall in love and marry a man because he has all the good qualities you don't have. After the wedding you find that those very qualities can be irritating. For example, Marvin's cheerful, sunny disposition is what I loved about him most, but when I am going through one of my trying, introspective, emotional times, I find his cheerfulness irritating. That is wrong of me, but it is honest. If we could grasp the divine way we are placed in families, we would see the necessity for each of our strengths, and we could forgive and even laugh at each others' weaknesses. I don't know all the answers, but I know that I am enjoying my dad just as he is, and I think he enjoys me too.

About the note. Characteristically, not a word has been spoken about it between Dad and me, and that's okay with me. The wall is down and who needs to discuss it? Well, I guess the person who is writing this book might feel a need to discuss it. But I have stopped trying to prove that I am anything but that little girl my parents love who grew up to be someone so special in God's eyes that before the foundation of the world He had provided for my eternity. Now that is security!

I will never forget the day when Mom and Dad returned to Kentucky after my suicide attempt. Dad slipped a check for a rather large amount into my hand before they left and said, "This is just for you, and if life ever gets to be too much for you, I will come and get you and bring you home." Is there healing in a get-well card? You bet there is, especially if it is from your daddy. Maybe a get-well card should be sent to all those in your family. An assurance of love is needed so often, and it can be preventive medicine.

If you have children and sometimes wonder how you are affecting them, you might receive some insight from the message on a little card I found one day.

CHILDREN LEARN WHAT THEY LIVE

If a child lives with criticism, he learns to condemn.
If a child lives with hostility, he learns to fight.
If a child lives with ridicule, he learns to be shy.
If a child lives with shame, he learns to feel guilty.
If a child lives with tolerance, he learns to be patient.
If a child lives with encouragement, he learns
   confidence.
If a child lives with praise, he learns to appreciate.
If a child lives with fairness, he learns justice.
If a child lives with security, he learns to have faith.
If a child lives with approval, he learns to like himself.
If a child lives with acceptance and friendship, he
   learns to find love in the world.*

*Author Unknown

FIVE

"How Could You on Easter?"

In Vine Grove, Kentucky, March 30, 1975, began with a crisp, windy sunrise service at a local church and evolved into a clear, sunny Easter Sunday.

My mom visited with her friends of thirty years at the Methodist church before singing the opening hymn, "He Arose."

Mom always had her spirits lifted by church, and this day was especially joyous as she stopped and counted her blessings. Yes, she was blessed indeed. She hummed softly as she prepared Sunday dinner for my daddy. After dinner Daddy went in the den to read the paper, and Mom went into the back bedroom for a short nap.

At about three o'clock the phone rang. Mom answered it there in the bedroom, anticipating the weekly call from my sister or me. Through multiplied long distance calls, she kept her hand on the pulse of both our lives. We teased her about dying some day with her fingers in the dial position. Daddy, of course, didn't hear her gasp when Marvin told her the grim news—that her oldest daughter had tried to commit suicide. Her stomach weakened and her throat tightened. The grief and agony of her soul were extreme. Holding her hands tightly together, she said to my daddy, "Well, Charles, we may very well lose our Marilee. She has tried to kill herself."

After giving him the details as she knew them, she slowly retreated to the bedroom.

Mom is as highly emotional and expressive as Daddy is cool and reserved. But when the real crises of life come to her, she seems endued with girders of steel.

Sorrow to anyone is an immensely personal thing, so much so that I have not asked either of my parents to relive those torturous days and hours that I might record them. They are forever recorded in the inner recesses of their minds and hearts; to ask them to replay them would be far too painful.

One thing my mom did tell me was that she talked to the Lord she had trusted at the age of ten, saying, "Lord, You know me so well. I don't deserve any favors, and You know that when I make promises I don't always keep them. But I have no one to turn to except You, and I am asking You to save my girl." Having entrusted the matter to Him, she spent the next few crucial days with her head buried under a pillow. Marvin had told her it was useless for her to come. The horror of seeing her own flesh and blood reduced to machines and tubes would be too harsh. He had to tell her bluntly that a decision might have to be made as to how long I should be kept alive by machines. . . . She should wait. She knew he meant either I would get well and need her, or I would not and she would be coming to Alabama for a funeral.

My mom began to try to put the puzzle together. The first pieces were drawn from an experience the month before. She and Daddy were finishing their winter vacation in Florida when Marvin and I spent the night with them on the way to Tampa for a job interview. She was shocked by my gaunt appearance. I had lost so much weight that my clothes hung loosely. She was worried, but what could she do?

She backtracked further, to October 1974, when I had been sent to the University of Alabama Medical Center to find out the cause of my severe, long-lasting headaches. One day I went through a brain scan, or electroencephalogram (EEG)—an electrical test based on brain waves—and an arteriogram, an X-ray test given by making an incision in the groin and inserting dye into the artery for diagnosis of brain tumor.

The very next day I was given a glucose tolerance test, which involved removal of blood and urine every hour to measure the ability to reduce blood sugar levels at a normal rate.

The granddaddy of all tests came that same day, the pneumoencephalogram. This is a combined neurological and X-ray procedure where some of the spinal fluid is removed and air is injected into the spinal column for localization of brain tumors or aneurysm. I was totally prepared for the other tests and understood what they would do, but I had never heard of the last one. Nevertheless, I was not worried or nervous about it. It was so painful, though, that I got nauseated several times and threw up during the test. The discomfort to my head was so severe that it was nearly a week before I could sit upright without excruciating pain. I remember Mom's crying when she saw me. She determined that she would go home with me and stay until I got on my feet again.

As my health deteriorated so did my will to live. The tests had revealed no abnormality. I guess the doctors decided my pain was psychological so they decided to treat me as if I were mentally ill. I was put on a drug that nearly immobilized me, thorazine. That medication did take away my pain, but it also took away everything that was Marilee Horton. It was the beginning of the end. Depression became a way of life for me.

The puzzle was taking form. Mom remembered that I had encouraged her to go home after three weeks—that I was going to be fine. In fact, my family and I even made the trip to Kentucky for Thanksgiving that year. But I had begun to lie to everyone about how I really felt. I was not in pain, but something far worse was happening to me because of the drug thorazine. I had stopped becoming involved in things; I just sort of sat quietly and observed life. My personality was changed, from bubbly enthusiasm over life to grim resignation.

We had a quiet Christmas with our children at home. We played games, and I thought I was beginning to get back to normal. But then the dreariness of January and February crept upon me. By this time Mom and Daddy had gone to Florida.

While Mom was trying to complete the puzzle, she tried to blame herself. She thought my childhood had a lot to do with my insecurity, anxiety, and poor self image. That was hard for me to understand since I recalled pleasant memories. The only problem was that I couldn't remember before the time I was eight years old.

I could remember vividly moving by train from Rhinelander, Wisconsin, to Vine Grove, Kentucky, when my daddy had served his time in the army and then went to work at Fort Knox as a civilian. Vine Grove was then a sleepy, southern town of about 3,500 people where farmers gathered at storefronts of. the tree-lined main street — a town where black people still lived in a section called "nigger town," much to my horror.

I had never seen a black child before that summer of 1946 when we moved into our apartment over the drugstore. I remember peering out the window at a little black boy licking earnestly an orange popsicle. There had been one black man in Rhinelander and he had worn a uniform and worked in the barber shop. I had never given much consideration to the plight of minority groups, but something began waking up inside of me about the equality of man.

I could never understand or appreciate the fact that black people had to eat in the back room of the one restaurant or drink from a separate fountain and go to a different school. I soon found that it wouldn't do for a newcomer to question those things, especially if she was just eight years old.

I acclimatized rapidly to this little town so different from the cool, snowy resort town in Wisconsin. Certainly no one vacationed in Vine Grove, but that was fine with me because it became my town. I loved to amble up the main street, stopping at store windows, pressing my nose to the glass, and peering into darkened and cool interiors of stores. They were filled not with expensive ski wear, fishing gear, and boats, but with colorful bolts of calicoes and ginghams suitable for school clothes and house dresses. People moved more slowly and smiled more often back then. Little children wore shorts and gaily ran barefoot in the streets. The drugstore was the hub of all activity during the summer when school was out.

There was no terror or fear in the town of my childhood. Doors remained unlocked and crime was unheard of, aside from petty shoplifting and minor disturbances of the peace. An occasional drunk graced the one jail cell that sat out in open space behind the "City Cafe." Nearly every Monday afternoon my friends and I would walk down the alley to see who was "in the clink," as Daddy called it. Often we would tease and point at the poor unfortunate soul who was stuck out for all to see. It has often reminded me of the stocks where people were incarcerated for public display in years gone by.

The only other fear I remember from my childhood was a poor, pitiful hunched creature I'll call Bobbie Hoe. To my knowledge he never hurt a soul, but my friends and I conjured up tales that would raise the hair on our arms. When any of us girls spent the night together, we would huddle under a blanket, no matter what the temperature, and whisper: "Bobbie Hoe is looking in the window." As far as I know Bobbie was severely retarded but harmless. More often than I can remember, Nellie, my best friend, and I would run, lickety split, home from the movie and jump in bed, just sure that Bobbie had limped all the way home and was lurking in the shadows under the old maple tree in her front yard. My days were filled with childish fun, problems, and pranks. My school experiences were nearly all very good.

Mom still can't understand why I don't remember my years before then. She says she thinks they may be blocked out for some reason by painful memories. They were years when my daddy was in the army and out of the country . . . years when a beautiful young mother had to work in a veneer factory and leave her only child with various keepers . . . days when the terrors of war could at any time make her a widow. Did her fears and insecurities become mine? I don't know.

Even memories of a dear grandmother and grandfather on Daddy's side are very dim during those years. I know that I must have been loved as the first grandchild, and one of the proofs of that love was the fierce envy of their youngest daughter, my Daddy's sister, Carolyn, who was just five years older than I. I didn't understand that jealousy until the age of eight when a little sister, Sherry, entered my life and sort of edged me off Mom's lap and into some sincere growing up.

My early spiritual training came as a result of my Mom's taking stock of what constituted proper raising of youngsters and concluding that church attendance had a place. The Lord was directing her life and had been since the young age when she placed her trust in Him.

As the three of us "girls" went to church, Mom began to grow in the Spirit and take a real place of responsibility in the community. She was soon in the middle of school, church, and community affairs. She was even elected council woman. My sister, Sherry, and I took our places in Sunday school, youth meetings, and choir. I look back on my church experiences as very solid and good. My only regret is that I was so slow in understanding that it was not my church attendance, Bible reading, and prayers that made me acceptable to God.

I was twenty-seven when all my good works were dashed to my feet and in spiritual nakedness I stood before God and claimed Christ as my Savior, apart from anything I could do. Mom was naturally surprised that I had "heard" for all those years and had never really experienced the new birth. I think she has always felt I held her responsible, but I really think we are saved according to God's timetable. It is His Spirit that draws us.

But why would one with new life years later choose self-inflicted death? The answer to that is still not complete, but it helps to remember that emotional healing is still necessary *after* spiritual healing. Spiritual rebirth does not guarantee the elimination of problems.

It is difficult for me to remember my mom any way but the way she is now. She is five feet, two inches tall and a little on the plump side but with beautiful legs, a result of walking up and down the hills that constitute our town as she helps care for folks who need her. She has lovely, full-bodied, gray hair that frames a slightly mischievous face. Daddy calls her "Peck's bad boy," whatever that means. It fits somehow. Her bright eyes don't miss a trick.

Mom is well read and very conversant in current events. She can intelligently address herself to almost any subject, and she won't turn down a good argument. She started college at forty and loved her classes and new friends. She is a very good wife and mother and provided me with a strong role model.

"You must always have a nice hot meal on the table when your husband gets home," she always advised me.

As my mother has aged, she has not withered but ripened. Young women still delight in her company, which is a tremendous compliment. She causes happiness and interest wherever she is. Whether on the campground with my retired daddy or in the midst of her much loved grandchildren, she is the current version of Mary Poppins. From the time my kids knew anything, they knew that she had grand and glorious things stuffed into her bag. She is the "Lollipop Queen" and is the only one in the running for the "Gold Popsicle" award. She is a firm believer that grandmothers are not meant to be practical or sensible, which used to drive Marvin and me crazy. She reminds me a little of Marie Antoinette when she says, "Let them eat ice cream." And she says that at breakfast! Her motto is "All they want, whenever they want." Her creed is: "They can eat normal food when I'm not here; I want them to have a little craziness and silliness in their lives." She will spend an enormous amount on food that would give health food fans the gastronomical vapors. But it brings squeals of delight from the junior section of my house.

There were times when we thought we weren't proper parents if we didn't protest such nonsense. But we soon saw that we were cheating our children out of a grandmother that any kid in the world would love to have. Besides, squelching that little gray bomb is no easy task. She has to show her love. She is not dishonest, but she believes the old adage "All's fair in love and war." She loves those kids and if it causes war with anyone, she's game. She twinkles as she sneaks Twinkies under the table and hides Doritos under their pillows. The more I see, the more I pray, "Lord I don't think I want to be a sensible grandma; let me be like Mom."

How does such a mother react when her own offspring tries to check out of life? Should she blame herself, especially if she also happens to be her daughter's best friend? I suppose her strange reaction to my death wish could have been predicted.

Mom had managed to pull herself from a troubled and poor childhood by making other people happy, and she found incredible strength in doing that. She has always managed to keep on keeping on. She wouldn't dream of giving up. What is that extra ingredient that she had and I didn't? I am still trying to figure that out. My hope is that the ingredient is there, dormant, just waiting for a grandbaby to wake it up.

After the first heartrending days she felt anger and was able to say: "How could you on Easter? I can never look at an Easter egg again." Her question was born out of the shock that anyone who had been in on *her* life could turn out to be so selfish—hurting other people in order to spare oneself more hurt.

Believe it or not, I really understand that. It is true. I did not have to be reminded of her love. I was sure she loved me. But the Lord has used her question to remind me of His love.

How could I mar the day of Christ's resurrection? I pray: "Lord, thanks for my mom. Help me be more like her and so wrap myself up in the lives of those I love that I wouldn't dare want to miss anything by leaving."

Mom has been a good picture of God's unconditional love and forgiveness as she picks me up, dusts me off, and helps me start all over again. And I know she really understands.

SIX

For Better or Worse

The days spent in the sterile quiet of the hospital room caused me to dig into my memory for clues to my near-fatal behavior.

I have no brothers and only one dear sister who is eight years younger than I. Sherry was a bright-eyed ten-year-old when I married, and because of the age difference and the many miles that separate us we have never had the opportunity to be as close as we would like. While still dealing with her own particular grief of nearly losing her sister, she called Mom from her home in Alexandria, Virginia, and asked, "Is there something wrong in their marriage?"

I wondered how many others mused over thoughts of a dissolving relationship or unfaithfulness. Marital problems drive many to suicide every day, but that was not my case.

I met Marvin when I was fourteen. I was just a foolish, giddy schoolgirl, jostling down the hall at our local high school, when I made the grand error of all time. I stepped on the spit-polished shoes of a crew-cut, jean-clad boy. (I often remember this incident of twenty-six years ago as I watch him shine all the shoes in our house on Saturday evenings. His reaction to my carelessness was a real clue to his personality and habits. Neat!)

He had no kind words for me that day, but that was just the beginning. I certainly didn't care then if our paths ever crossed again. However, in a high school of 250 that would have been highly unlikely. A funny thing began happening at the ballgames. I saved a seat for a lanky, good-looking junior varsity basketball player time after time, only to have Marvin Horton, always cheerful and eternally optimistic, plop himself down in it before the other boy could shower and get to the bleachers. At first I was so aggravated I could have chewed a nail in two. I don't really remember just when I began to take an interest in the green-eyed, brown-haired handsome hillbilly, but before I was sixteen I was certain I wanted to spend the rest of my life with him.

Our dating years were happy, but our year-long engagement was torturous because of his attending school in Nashville. Our dating had mostly centered around church activities, mainly because they were free and Marvin was poor, but also because he had made a real commitment to Jesus Christ when he was fifteen. As far as we both knew then, I too was a Christian. I did all the right things, but I knew deep down that he had a peace and joy that was not genuine with me. Emptiness would have better described my inner condition.

Finally the day we had long anticipated broke through the long night of waiting. It was a frosty gray February 9. The bare trees seemed to bow before us as we drove to the church. Our wedding was the first held in our small town's beautiful new Methodist church, and everyone thought the ceremony was gorgeous. The bridesmaids wore red taffeta with white fur muffs, and I wore a very simply styled gown of elegant embroidered heavy satin.

I would be lying if I said the day was all that I had unrealistically dreamed of. It was not romantic or sentimental as I had hoped; rather it was a bittersweet "last day" at home, with out-of-town guests spilling in and out of our small house all day in a general party mood. A couple of times I shed tears for my passing childhood. Sherry cried when it dawned on her that having the room to herself was not nearly the victory she had thought it would be.

Like most brides, I was so carried away by logistics that it seemed I was planning for everyone's happiness but ours. It was hard for me to enjoy the coming event, especially through a negative, melancholy temperament that foresaw me tripping on my train and falling into the cake. But Marvin and I survived the wedding as do most couples, and finally got away to ourselves. Then we knew it had all been worth it.

We went to my birthplace for our honeymoon. I guess it's sort of strange to visit grandparents on a honeymoon, but I was so proud of my "catch" that I wanted all my relatives to meet and love him too. Rhinelander, Wisconsin, is snowy and cold in February, but we hardly noticed, so warm was the newness of fulfilled love. I was so happy that I had a continuous, pleasant lump in my throat and flutters in my stomach. Not yet realizing the full impact of God's role in our marriage, I believed with all my heart that it was made in heaven.

Our first home was a tiny trailer where a neat country boy set out to teach a messy Yankee girl how to cook such staples as pinto beans and cornbread.

Whereupon the city girl introduced the country boy to such things as mushrooms and oysters, which we could ill afford on thirty-five dollars a week. I had learned to cook really well at Mom's side, but after surviving the Depression my parents had decided not to skimp on food, so I was used to the best. Much to the shock of my neat and clean husband, my cooking style had the same flair as Mom's. Mom and I never measure anything; sort of an innate sense about how much, how long, and how hot belongs to us. We leave a colossal mess behind. We experiment a lot and love to serve our food to guests. I think cooking is the one phase of homemaking I most enjoy.

The difference in the way Marvin and I do things can be seen in the making of a sandwich. He methodically removes all the ingredients from the refrigerator, builds his sandwich, places it on a plate, and then proceeds to put everything back into place. He even wipes off the counter before he eats. On the other hand, I remove what I need as the need strikes me, one by one. I leave jar covers off, and I don't put anything back until after I have consumed my sandwich, which usually happens before I can sit down.

Our marriage was built upon the old-fashioned, fairy tale love that was to glue two opposites together so strongly that the storms of adversity, the winds of affliction, and the rains of confusion could not cause a separation.

Two baby boys came within a nineteen-month period, and the act of trying to balance my new responsibilities so that the marriage relationship stayed in its rightful place was not easy. I was not easy to live with either during this time. I began to question, "Is this all there is to marriage?" "Is this all there is to motherhood?"

Ever in search of fulfillment, I went to work for a research firm on a military base. Working with psychologists who were using everything from laser beams to hypnosis in connection with training combat soldiers was mentally very stimulating. I developed inflated ideas about my capacity for a career. I digested hungrily any books on psychology I could get my hands on.

The only seriously troublesome period in our marriage occurred at this time. I had taken entrance exams at the University of Kentucky, and I found that almost anything was more fun than going home to squabbling children and a Mt. Everest stack of laundry. I began to neglect my marriage and my home as I toyed with alcohol and a life-style contrary to the ground rules we had laid. More and more I screamed for my freedom. But the more I stretched out from under the protective umbrella of my husband, the more miserable I was. I was becoming anxious and deeply troubled about my purpose in the world.

The defense for my freedom was toppled upon discovery of my third pregnancy. As usual, I became happily domestic and satisfied during that time. The change in my attitude was so welcome that Marvin forgave old hurts, and we became content again. It was new and exciting caring for the little girl we had dreamed of—dresses instead of jeans, dolls instead of cars.

Marvin and I were becoming Mr. and Mrs.

Average American when trouble hit again. Not only was I still chomping at the bit for my fulfillment, but Marvin was beginning to expand a little on his own. I call it "vocational vacillation." In common language the term means "the grass is always greener on the other side of the fence." I had taken it in stride when after completing diesel school and working for a heavy equipment firm, Marvin hurt his back and took another job at a safety equipment company. Within a couple of years he decided he wanted to move up from stock boy to salesman. His boss didn't agree, however, so Marvin quit and opened his own safety equipment business with me as his only employee. My bookkeeping chores ran into the wee hours of the morning, but I was content to help him get a start.

As he became more proficient in the ways of making money, more and more opportunities opened up and he felt constrained to try them all. The one that caused the most trouble came about three years after our baby girl, Mandi, was born. Marvin was restless and wanted to set out for the big pot at the end of the rainbow. He had the opportunity to invest in the bottom floor of a new life insurance company that would necessitate our moving to Alabama.

I was torn apart like confetti—we suffered our first and only separation as he doggedly and determinedly removed all of our savings, borrowed money from banks and friends, and went to Alabama.

I was just as determined to remain in the "squatter's rights" position, keep the kids in school, and wait for this new venture to wear off. I must say that I carried this off in true martyr fashion for about six months. Many weekends Marvin would drive the seven- or eight-hour trip home; his eyes were blood-shot and our visits were strained. I was very resentful of the fact that I was seemingly raising the children alone while he seemed to be having the time of his life. Many weeks we would only be able to have a brief rendezvous in some bar when he was between planes. He would flash great wads of money that people had trusted to him to invest.

There were several factors involved that made me change my mind about joining him. One was pity—he was very weary of traveling back and forth and he did love his family. Another one was greed. The great wads of green bills seemed to fortify his predic-tion: "Baby, this time we are going to make it big." But the main factor was that I genuinely loved him, and deep within I knew we had one of the few marriages that had possibilities of being great, in spite of all the differences.

So I went through the gruesome process of trying to keep a house filled with little children clean in order to show it and sell it, which we weren't able to do for years.

Sale or no, we U-Hauled our family from Louisville to Birmingham on New Year's Eve, 1965. "What a way to usher in the new year," was my thought.

Six months after moving to the city of steel mills and hills adorned with dogwoods and rainbow-colored azaleas, what I knew deep in my old melan-choly heart would happen did happen. The bottom fell out of the "this is it, baby" business, and we received only ten cents back on each hard earned or borrowed dollar, leaving us deeply and desperately in debt. Most grevious were debts to our good friends who had loaned as much as $10,000 without even a note.

That spring of 1966 was very bleak. The beautiful blossoms didn't bloom for me. I was flying apart inside and I wanted to scream; instead I held it in and tried to pray. But the God of my childhood had vanished as might a puff of smoke. How I wished I hadn't been playing church every Sunday of my life up to this point. That was all it had been—play. There was no reality to Christianity as I knew it, not in a crisis. The fellowship suppers were fun, the songs the choir sang were beautiful, but somehow I had missed the mark. Jesus Christ was not a part of my life, and I almost wanted to curse Him. It seemed He had hidden the way from me and was now punishing me for being lost. I hated everything and everyone, yes, even God Himself. Wanting to die but lacking the guts, I just went on living day after dreary day without hope.

Too broke to get back to Kentucky and too poor to even drown my sorrows in demon rum, there was only one alternative—work! I was able to pull off my great imposter act and land a very good job as office manager for two dentists in one of the most exclusive practices in town. I convinced them that while I was not the college graduate they had advertised for, I had plenty of experience in efficiently dealing with the public and professionals and could put some know-it-all college kid to shame. I answered their ad with a letter to that effect, which even I thought was rude, and I never seriously expected to hear from them. But they called and said they liked my spunk and offered me the job.

The late night burning of the oil while studying dentistry brought a certain healing and purpose to my life. I didn't know an amalgam filling from a prophylactic exam, but I knew how to check books out of the library. Before long I was taking patients into a private office and explaining in great detail just what the doctor planned to do and how they could finance it. And in that type of practice, the cost of the work done was rarely under what I considered a fortune.

Also about this time, Marvin, with his usual propensity for adventure, landed what he called the "sweetest job in town" as a candy salesman. He called mainly on schools that were interested in fund raising. And of course he was enjoying the present to the hilt; there was no time for crying over spilled milk. Planning for the future was not his bag. All the while I was shaking my head and asking, "Who wants to buy candy? It won't last!"

This new job moved us again—deeper into the interior of Alabama. If that sounds like a missionary inching his way into the jungle of Africa, then I have gotten across how I felt. I, of course, gave up my interesting job and felt bitter resentment about that. I stoically covered my feelings as I smiled sweetly at the neighbors in a lovely neighborhood in Prattville, Alabama, where somehow we had managed to purchase another home, larger and newer than before.

The big game started all over again—lovely home, fancy church, all the right parties; but I was a shambles, and a certain death had begun in me as I pondered the age-old question: "Why was I born?"

Or as Job said, "Why did I not die at birth, Come forth from the womb and expire?" (Job 3:11).

Our marriage vows had included "for better or for worse"; I wondered if it would ever get better. Inwardly, however, I knew it wasn't my marriage that was "worse"—it was me, so how was I to get "better"?

I still marvel at all the great pains God took and all the maneuvering He did to get us just where He wanted us and in just the condition He wanted us. A psychiatrist that I consulted about the drinking which had become troublesome to me made an interesting statement. He deducted after our first session that my state was "lost" and "lonely." That was exactly how I felt, but what was I to do about it? I was mentally at the bottom of the heap.

After my visit to the psychiatrist, someone visited me. It was George O'Brian, a young minister, who called at our home and shared the gospel with me. At first I was amazed at the gall of someone actually telling me that God loved me. The psychiatrist had said I felt alienated from the whole world and hostile toward it; so, how could anyone love me? Then I was shaken that the minister made the same deduction about me the psychiatrist had—"lost" and "lonely." I was lost because of my sin, which I was almost glad to acknowledge to someone. It seemed everyone was living the fractured way I was and was not troubled by it, thus to them it was not sin. But there it was in black and white: ". . . All have sinned and fall short of the glory of God" (Rom. 3:23). Pastor O'Brian said I was lonely because I was separated from the God who had created me to have fellowship with Him. He said God loved me and so had sent His only perfect, sinless Son to die on the cross in my place. That Jesus was raised on the third day is proof of God's acceptance of Christ's sacrifice. I had heard the gist of this before but not in a personal way, a way that included me.

My heart was touched by the love and gentleness that spilled out from this man's eyes as he sweetly tried to lead me into a relationship with his Savior, Jesus Christ. While moved by someone caring enough to want to help me, my heart was hardened to the point that I just couldn't believe. "It's just too simple," I said as I showed him out. I knew his spirit was heavy because his shoulders sagged some and his gait was not as sprightly as when he had entered. I almost felt as sorry for him as I did for myself.

The minister left a little gospel tract with me that gave the same plan of salvation that we had discussed, and I literally wore it out reading and trying to believe.

The dullness of my once quick mind bothered me. I was paying fifty dollars an hour to talk to a psychiatrist who didn't really care about my troubles, and who didn't seem to have any answers other than to tell me how depressed I was. I knew that already!

On the other hand, this minister seemed to have a genuine concern for me and his joy seemed to come from any progress I made toward the Lord. He focused on solutions rather than problems, and his advice was free! My own stupidity was reinforced by Satan's hurling doubts into my mind as I read such books as *The Passover Plot*, which raised questions about the validity of the Resurrection. I was also very confused about heaven and hell. Were these places real? Or was the gospel the biggest lie in the world?

Time and time again the minister would come with the Word of God and apply it to whatever the reigning doubt of the day was, much like a bandage for an open wound. I wondered at his persistence in spite of my rejections. Why didn't he give up? Everyone else had, I thought.

The more I rejected the more wretched I became. Life had lost all purpose. I was desperately trying to be a good wife and mother, but I was totally disappointed—in my marriage, my children, the material gain that had brought me no happiness, but mostly in myself and my inability to be content and happy. What was wrong with me? I had stopped looking for the pot at the end of the rainbow; in fact, I somehow knew that whatever was at the end of anyone's rainbow would not fill the longing in my heart. So I stopped looking even for the rainbow; all my goals were unattainable. Then came that orange and red day in October.

I awakened with the same dreadful fear in my heart that I just couldn't get through the day. But I swung my long, thin legs over the side of the bed and stared at myself in the dresser mirror. "Oh yes you can; you can make a go of it," I lied to myself. "Today I will give up drinking. I *will* be a good wife and mother. I *will* straighten out my life, and I *will* even go to that man's church." That is what it means to pull one's self up by the bootstraps (and I had had enough of that cliché to last everyone who ever intended to wear boots).

So I began the day with purpose and determination. I even smiled and gritted my teeth instead of yelling at the children. But then dusk fell like a gray, lace shawl around my soul, and I felt panic. I had to have a drink; I thought I would go crazy without it. So I gave in. I thought it would ease the pain as the black shroud of night crept over all, but it didn't help and I was desperate. I got out the little worn, pink gospel tract and read again, "For God so loved the world, that He gave His only begotten Son . . ." (John 3:16). But this time it seemed to read, "For God so loved Marilee Horton. . . ." A tiny, tiny glimmer of light squeezed into my heart and through copious tears it grew and grew until I cried out in the most exquisite relief: "Dear Jesus, I will never understand how You could love one such as I, but You have given me that one seed of faith and I believe it. Please come into my heart and life. I have made a mess of my life and if You want me, You can have me. I am sorry I have sinned against You. I want You to be my Savior and control my life."

Bells didn't ring, lights didn't flash, and I didn't tingle all over; but what I had been searching for all my life happened in an instant. A peace flooded my soul, and it was indeed welcome. Inside my body, frail from weeks of not eating properly, a spiritual healing was taking place. God spoke to my heart in a gentle voice only audible now because His Spirit and mine could communicate, and He said, "Everything is going to be all right." That is all He said, but a calm assurance came that Jesus had lifted my burden of sin and guilt and I was free at last.

Some have said that I went from one crutch to another and in a way that is true, but Christianity is called a yoke instead of a crutch. Matthew 11:28–30 says: "Come unto me, all ye that labor and are heavy laden, and I will give you rest. Take my yoke upon you, and learn of me; for I am meek and lowly in heart: and ye shall find rest unto your souls. For my yoke is easy, and my burden is light" (KJV).

Alcohol had been a crutch, but even that had given away and I was left helpless. When I took upon myself the yoke of Jesus, how precious it was to see that a yoke has places for two so you need not walk alone. I was not alone anymore.

I didn't know it then, but there was rejoicing in heaven over my being found. I was rejoicing too, but how was I going to convince my husband the "worse" part of the contract was over and the "better" was on the way? Contrary to my usual conniving ways, I decided to let Jesus convince my family, and I really rested that night. Oh how sweet!

SEVEN

For Richer or Poorer

The next morning I stretched lazily like an old cat and blinked a couple of times before looking at the clock on the bedside table. Seven hours had passed, and I felt like Rip Van Winkle in reverse. I felt seven years younger, and for the first time in a long time I was actually glad to see the sun peeking through the slit in the green damask draperies. I wanted to leap up, throw open the window, and reach out and hug the fragrant, blossoming gardenia bush just outside our window.

Oh! I was a new woman. I had forgotten there was a world full of flowers for me to smell. The birds were humming and singing as if giving a command performance just for me. I didn't know the proper words for Christian praise such as "hallelujah" or "praise the Lord"; I just kept whispering "thank You" over and over again. Somehow I knew God accepted that as the highest worship I was probably ever to offer.

I was indeed grateful. Suddenly I realized that the angry fist that clenched my stomach every morning was gone. I was content. In fact, all my morning regulars had evidently found someone else to trouble. They were gone—fear, panic, dread, foreboding, and the plaguing depression and weariness. (However, unknown to me these evil spirits who left me knew there would come a time when they could return, and if I hadn't learned how to resist, I would be in trouble.)

I had even actually slept well for the first time in years. Then I remembered the verse in the tract that I had worn thin: "Come unto me, all ye that labor and are heavy laden, and I will give you rest" (Matt. 11:28). All at once I knew—it was Jesus! He was just as real in my soul as the sun streaming in the window. I had ceased my labor the night before as I came to the end of myself and laid my heavy burden of sin down at His precious feet. And He had given the rest He promised.

I stifled the impulse I had to sing. Parts of an old hymn from my childhood filled my heart; a favorite of a dear, godly old lady who had worked with the youth in our church:

> I come to the garden alone,
> While the dew is still on the roses,
> And the voice I hear, falling on my ear,
> The Son of God discloses.
>
> And He walks with me,
> And He talks with me,
> And He tells me I am His own;
> And the joy we share as we tarry there,
> None other has ever known.
>
> He speaks, and the sound of His voice
> Is so sweet the birds hush their singing,
> And the melody
> That He gave to me,
> Within my heart is ringing.*

—C. Austin Miles

For the first time I understood why she wanted to sing that song every Sunday night. The words were as clear a message as I knew that He was giving me that melody. One reason I was shy about just bursting into song was that Marvin would have had a stroke. His morning cheerfulness, his whistling and singing nearly drove me up the wall. I usually couldn't even work up a good growl before the coffee was surging through my system. Now something new and great was happening. Bits and pieces of another song flew into my mind: "Though Christ hath regarded my helpless estate, and hath shed His own blood for my soul . . . It is well, it is well with my soul" (by H. G. Spafford and P. P. Bliss).

While I was basking in the new-found love of the great Forgiver, my mind naturally turned to the strong, warm body lying next to me. "Could he forgive me, too?" I knew he would, because in spite of all that we had been through, and while I knew he didn't understand my complexities, I did know without a shadow of a doubt that he loved me.

How could he? I had often been perplexed by his unconditional love. It was a godly trait, just as was his great capacity to forgive time and time again.

Scales were slipping off my eyes as I realized that because God did live within Marvin he could love and forgive just as Christ did. Being a Christian had given him the grace to continue in a slightly one-sided relationship. He did nearly all the giving, and I began to see how completely self-centered and spoiled I had been.

I was almost overcome by grief as I realized how I had hurt him, and a tiny sob escaped from my tight throat. Within a second, I was in his strong arms and he rocked me back and forth saying, "Honey, what's wrong?" Finally, through a vast profusion of hot tears, I smiled, "Nothing, nothing is wrong anymore; everything is all right." He raised on one elbow, tenderly gazed into my teary eyes, and asked, "What do you mean?" I knew he was trying to gain some understanding of my confusing personality changes, and he probably thought he was in for a new twist. He looked stunned momentarily as I said, "Oh, Honey, I have accepted Jesus. He has given me peace, and I'm so happy." As I struggled with that word "happy," I began sobbing again, only this time big tears were rolling down his cheeks, too. That morning was the beginning of a real marriage for us.

Just as the Word of the Lord promised, I did get better, and the Lord Jesus convinced everyone who ever knew me that a change had taken place. Old things really were passing away and all things were new. Marvin and I discussed the fact that he had been a Christian from age fifteen and had not realized that I was not. But the "one rotten apple in the barrel" story helped us to see that by his giving in to what I wanted to do instead of sticking to his principles and growing in Christ, he had gotten as far out of fellowship with the Lord as possible. As we began to attend a church where the Scriptures were clearly taught, Marvin understood that he had never grown as a Christian. He was still a baby, just like me, and as two brand new babies we began to drink the milk of the Word of God and grow.

We had to learn to talk all over again. Complaining and swearing, yelling and murmuring, all had to be replaced with spiritual songs, hymns, and psalms, gentleness and kindness. It was a good changing process, but not easy or rapid.

I shall never forget the night Marvin brought home two new, leather study Bibles, and we sat in the middle of the bed and started in Genesis reading and saying, "Hey, look at this." "Well, I never knew this; here is a word picture of the Lord Jesus Christ, right in the beginning of the Scriptures!" Those were precious days indeed.

Seeing my family through the eyes of the Lord changed my attitude toward them and toward all my responsibilities. It was exciting to see the children trust Christ as Savior early, before a life of desperation. It was also exciting to see Marvin commit his entire life to the Lord, even the candy business. I didn't think anyone would buy candy, but when the Lord took over that candy business, we couldn't fill orders fast enough. Somehow we knew the Lord was getting us out of debt and back on the solvent side of the road for a purpose other than being rich. We didn't know just what He would do, but we trusted Him.

Our family became the strong unit God meant for it to be, based on biblical principles. No longer did I have to ask, "Is this all there is?" There was so much I couldn't contain it all. As some of it spilled over, we saw many of our neighbors come to Christ; and a life of witnessing began.

As we learned the principles taught in the Word about the lordship of Christ and the chain of command for the family, things began to make sense. I took my rightful place under the protective umbrella of my husband, and our marriage took on a whole new dimension. It was very comfortable, for a change, to trust God to work through my husband. It was surprising to me to find out that God didn't necessarily need me as a go-between, either. He had the Holy Spirit who was perfectly capable of teaching my husband. I finally learned to duck, with mouth closed, and the Lord would hit Marvin smack between the eyes with whatever message He wanted him to have. I knew the Lord was trying to teach me to trust Him through trusting my husband. That has been a difficult lesson, and I haven't received a diploma yet.

Our relationship with the children began to change. We learned to use the Bible as a training manual for raising children and it worked as nothing else ever had.

Now, I have heard many glowing accounts similar to mine, after which the lovely lady sits down with a wonderful smile and you are led to believe that she and her family lived happily ever after. But having been disappointed in myself time and time again for not being in that sublimely happy state those "testimony women" seemed to have achieved, I have decided to come clean. None of us, and especially me, have arrived yet. If we are all honest, we will admit that though we are well on our way, we are not there yet. Philippians 3:13 reads, "Brethren, I do not regard myself as having laid hold of it yet; but one thing I do: forgetting what lies behind and reaching forward to what lies ahead, I press on . . ."

I have found it extremely difficult, as a strongly opinionated, high-strung, creative woman, to say, "I will submit to the authority of my husband" in accordance with Ephesians 5:22. It still isn't easy, but I can say that when I obey God in this matter He always blesses.

Mind you, I am no doormat, nor does an intelligent man like my husband have need of a doormat. He wanted a wife to share life with and that is what we do. Many times my suggestions are better than his, and he is no less a man for acknowledging that. It has built my character considerably, however, to admit that many times his suggestions are better than mine.

Whenever we discuss things loudly, and we do, we remember: "If two people say they never disagree, one of them is unnecessary." But I have learned the Philippians 3:13 principle well, because first God has forgiven and *forgotten* my sin and next Marvin was a picture of God to me by forgiving and *forgetting* my wrongs.

Now, no matter what transpires, I look at the calendar each morning and as I look at the date for the previous day, I say, "Lord, that day is gone. I have won some victories and I have made some blunders. Thank You for forgiving me; now as I turn the page let's start on a new day together. Thank You that Your mercies are new every morning."

If I had only learned that principle earlier in life it would have saved a lot of bitterness. Forgive, forget, and forge ahead.

There are differences between Marvin and me that are hard to adjust to. Marvin still loves adventure and I still love stability. If I had had my way, he would probably be nearing retirement as a stockboy in Louisville and receiving a watch for all his boring years. Yuck! That does have a dreary ring to it! Sure I get scared when he wants to try something new. But I can say I have never been bored. I have been to a lot of wonderful places and met a lot of wonderful people just because Marvin kept moving on.

There have been some really weird, risky business ventures that I stubbornly dug my number seven-and-a-half shoes in the ground and wouldn't budge on because I thought they were wrong. Marvin has come to trust my gift for discernment as I have come to trust him to provide amply for his family.

As I mentioned before, all of our troubles didn't just vanish because we trusted Christ as our Savior. But He began to set things in order as we got our priorities straight.

I think Marvin was absolutely, positively sure I was a new creature when one Sunday shortly after my salvation on a drive in the country I spotted a tiny, little old house set back off the road that was for sale, and I wanted it. Before I had always wanted the newest and best, but all our new homes and cars had not brought me peace and had put us incredibly in debt. As we walked on the porch of this little house, I knew Marvin was thinking, "She must be nuts!" Before I even went into that house, which was built only as high as the little man who built it could reach, God had given me a desire to live there. It was very small and very homemade and not at all attractive, but it was on the edge of a lush, green woods with red birds darting in and out. There was a spring down past the pig huts. The price for the house with all the out buildings (which were in really bad condition) and three acres (mostly hilly) was nine thousand dollars—the price of a really good car. But I wanted it, and I knew God was changing my wants.

We purchased that old house, contrary to every thing we had ever had and every way we had ever lived, and there we spent three of the most glorious, therapeutic years of our lives (1966–1969). I stopped working outside the home and began the hardest work of my life. We had a garden, planted in Marvin's usual enthusiasm, that was large enough to produce food for several families. Of course, the produce had to be picked, cleaned, and put up. We had pigs, large and small, goats, calves, and a very temporary flock of chickens. The chickens were around until one Saturday when, after killing, scalding, plucking, and cleaning twenty-two chickens, we gave the rest away. It was some time before we could even think about Colonel Sanders and licking our fingers.

We waded in the stream and screamed when we saw snakes. I hung clothes out and watched the red birds for hours. We nursed baby piglets and goats in our house when they took ill. We watched the children get muddy as they chanced to ride on one of the larger pigs and then settled on the little pinto pony we bought. Those three years brought healing to my mind, and our family gained a certain stability about why we were alive and who was in control of all nature. I could have stayed there forever, wearing the little homemade feed sack dresses that I thought pleased God for me to wear.

When I think of feed-sack dresses my memory takes a real humorous turn. I had always dressed fashionably with expensive clothes. I suppose the

way I looked comprised a big part of my life up until I
became a Christian.

I had always climbed rapidly up the secretarial
ladder in every place I worked, and that demanded
nice suits, shoes, and handbags. I had my hair done
every week and was carefully groomed on almost
every occasion.

On the October Sunday after my rebirth experience, my family and I trounced down to the little
Baptist church pastored by Brother George. I don't
know who was more shocked, the flock of thirty-five
who stared at me with my tweed and suede suit, my
hair piled high on my head, and enough make-up to
gussy up all the women in the building, or me as I
stared back at seventeen women who were the
epitome of plain. And what was worse—I knew they
were dressed up for Sunday.

I know the silence was only for my ears. Surely
they were burning the ears of God as they prayed for
such a worldly, painted floozy!

They were meeting in an old, tiny house and the
pulpit stood right in front of the kitchen sink. The
folding chairs squeaked and rattled every time you
moved and there was considerable movement with
our three children.

Once I got past the difference in our appearances,
I was in love with the people, the pastor, and the
place. (And remember I was the First Church type all
the way!) I saw the Lord in that place, and since I was
the only one at that time all duded up, I was sure they
were godly and I wasn't.

Those precious ladies used to laugh later when
they told how I looked with all that eye make-up on

and that hair on top of my head. I knew they were pleased as week by week I determined to be "godly" like them.

In a matter of weeks after we moved to the country I found it easy to become plain. I stopped working and kept house without the aid of the maids I had had before. I even went so far as to make some dresses for me and Mandi, and I don't sew!

By the time I had sunk into soft soil up to my mid-calf while planting a garden for the third time in one week, and after I had helped "string up" a calf for butchering, I knew "godly" was on the way.

The man we bought the farm from tried to teach us "city slickers" a few things about gardening. One day after he instructed me to go down the long, long rows of vegetable plants and thin them out, he stopped by and caught me saving the little green plants that I had culled out. He demanded to know what I was doing, and I cried as I told him I couldn't bear the thought of throwing them away. After all, I had almost given birth to them.

When I was a little girl we used to laugh at the girls who wore "feed-sack" dresses, but during my stay in the country I learned to regret that. One day Marvin was hauling sacks of feed in for the pigs and chickens and my beady eye spotted little purple pansies on an off-white background. An idea was born—what could be more "godly" than feed-sack dresses? Well, I was willing.

I know the Lord must have had a good laugh at me while I was going through spiritual infancy, thinking that I could tack on "godliness" by what I wore.

I also am grateful that the Lord has since shown me

that dressing beautifully can be as much a testimony to the goodness of God as dressing plainly. Being content with such things as we have is the secret.

It seems that all of those years were just special training ground for future service. As it became clear that God wanted us debt free, we were able, by selling our homes and selling tons of candy within eighteen months, to be solvent again and to pay back all of our friends and banks. The ultimate joy came during a period of special closeness as we prayed about what the Lord wanted us to do with the rest of our lives.

Our little four-and-one-half-year-old Mandi had been led to Christ by a dear woman who was the wife of the director for Child Evangelism Fellowship in our area. This ministry is specially dedicated to giving the gospel to children. She used the wonderful story of the Wordless Book (a book of colors, without words or pictures, which is used to tell the gospel). She shared Jesus Christ with Mandi who readily agreed that her heart was dark with sin like the black page. She wanted to one day go to heaven, represented by the gold page, and she trusted in the blood of Jesus (red page) to make her heart clean as the white page. Her subsequent growth was well-represented by the green page. We were so excited by the genuine belief that Mandi had experienced that we became volunteers for this work with children, having Bible Clubs and working at fairs. I found a wonderful niche in teaching flannelgraph Bible stories. I just came alive in front of the children. The Lord really spoke to Marvin about full-time service in this ministry, and our hearts were knit on the matter.

Marvin and I couldn't have been happier to discover our new attitude toward the "richer or poorer" part of our marriage vows. Stripped of many of the things we once held dear, we found ourselves overflowing with riches this world knows nothing of.

EIGHT

In Sickness and Health

It was a typical May day in Alabama—cool and crisp in the morning, warm and muggy by afternoon—when we packed up our three children and belongings into a VW van and headed for Muskegon, Michigan, in 1969. There was excitement and also apprehension about going back to school of any sort at our age, with a family to boot. Also, adding color to the picture, I was pregnant with our fourth child.

It was still frosty cold when we pulled into Muskegon and onto the grounds of the Child Evangelism Fellowship Institute where we were to receive our leadership training. But our hearts were warmed by the fellowship of students from all over the world who were interested in seeing boys and girls won to Jesus before their lives were marred by sin.

Our family was assigned a little three-room apartment, and our oldest son was given the joyous job of watching the other two children and keeping things from flying apart for the three months we were to be there. Those three months passed quickly as we were engrossed in the study of God's Word and the ways of being missionaries.

I had intended to fly home early in order to have the baby. However, the Lord impressed upon us that I should stay there and He would take care of all the things we had left undone, such as buying baby clothes, diapers, and bottles. It was a special time of trusting and not understanding God's dealings. I had especially looked forward to the peri-cervical delivery that the obstetrician in Alabama had planned. I was to be anesthetized early in labor and have a nearly painless delivery—something I had never enjoyed in birthing three big babies. In Michigan the Lord led us to a fine Christian physician, a dark, stocky, precious man, who didn't have too much to say about his method of relieving pain. But we continued to believe God had a purpose in my staying, even when the baby was late and we had only a little more than a week till graduation and then the one-thousand-mile trip home.

Finally, just seven days before graduation, the once-dreaded labor pains were welcomed as I thought, "Let's get this show on the road." Humming on the way to the hospital, I asked Marvin to stop so we could have a Coke; contrary to my worrywart nature I had no dismal foreboding about the precious cargo I was carrying.

A couple of hours into labor, however, and I knew I was on no picnic. Although they allowed Marvin in the labor room, he could really offer little comfort, and I nearly rubbed all the hair off his arm.

They certainly didn't believe in overdoing the drugs at that hospital. I wondered if the North were still trying to punish the South for something. I started to scream, "But I am a Yankee. I was born in Wisconsin!"

Finally, I was wheeled into the delivery room; relief was on the way, or so I thought. I had forgotten about the new painless methods—anything would have done.

I had usually had a saddle block and even looked forward to seeing that long needle. But when they strapped my feet in the stirrups I knew that was out. "What are you going to give me, gas?" The kindly, Christian man turned into Dr. Jekyll. His laughing eyes were hard. He didn't even answer me.

It would be a gross understatement to say I was uncomfortable. I had a long and difficult delivery with the physician fairly screaming at me to "PUSH!" It was a nightmare of the worst kind. I was sure God had made a dreadful mistake to let me suffer so, and I became angry at Him and at the doctor.

When it was finally all over and I had been given nothing for pain, only oxygen to keep me from passing out (which I would have gladly done), I was jerking so hard from pain reflexes I could hardly stay in my bed. I was in my room at 11:30 P.M., and all I knew was that I had had a boy.

The delivery room scene had been so different from the other three times that I felt something was wrong. In my three previous deliveries I had been awake; the doctor would tease me and the nurses would be filled with wonder as the miracle took place. This time it was grim, and I couldn't understand it.

When the doctor walked softly into my now darkened room, I was still shivering and very angry. When he entered, holding a chart, I said, "If I had known what you were going to do, I certainly would have gone back to Alabama to my own obstetrician!"

Back to his sweet self, the doctor, smiling, said,

"I'm sorry, but as you progressed in labor we knew there would be trouble. That baby had the largest shoulders of any baby I had ever delivered and the cord was around his neck. If we had given you any anesthesia, the birth canal would have relaxed and there wouldn't have been the time or strength for the push needed. If we had known earlier, I would have done a cesarean section. Had you gone and had the peri-cervical, your baby would have probably been born dead. As it is you have a healthy, nine-and-a-half pound boy. The Lord be praised."

I apologized to the doctor and thanked him.

As I lay in my bed I saw once again the hand of God. In obedience to the still small voice of His Spirit, I had stayed there to have my baby. I knew that had I gone on in stubbornness, not only would we probably have lost our baby, but Marvin wouldn't have graduated from the Institute. As it was, I borrowed a dress, and just five days after delivery, with baby watching, I marched across the stage and received my diploma too. There was a special little blue diploma made out to Matthew Horton for attending all the classes (prenatal).

I had had the last of my final exams in the labor room—learning to trust God even when it means pain and confusion for a time. I thanked God, and we knew that Matthew Paul would be our new son's name. It means "gift from God."

I am always moved when I remember the attention Matthew received. With all the work the students had to do and with what little money most of them had, they had made little quilts and a makeshift bed out of a plastic tub covered in quilted flannel. They bought disposable diapers and throwaway formula bottles. We lacked for nothing as God continued to teach us the truth of Philippians 4:19, "And my God shall supply all your need. . . ."

The trip home was also no picnic, but God's grace was certainly sufficient and His goodness sustained us. But somehow in the pit of our stomachs we knew when we pulled onto that old three-acre, dusty place in the country, we weren't there to stay. And in three months we were packed again.

Because of the need for a CEF director in a town in northern Alabama, we responded and moved to Gadsden. The first couple of times we went to look for a house, I hated the place. It was a steel mill town and a tire manufacturing center, and much of the town was grimy. Each time we consulted with the realtor, he showed us through the only house in town that would suit our needs for the paltry sum we could afford. It was a large old house with a hideous front porch, and for some reason I didn't like it. I would march through it and say, "This just won't do." I did that three times, and we knew we couldn't keep driving three hours back and forth to look at the same house. God was trying to tell me something, but my will was still very strong. Actually this house was much better than the one in the country, but it was in town, there was no property with it, and I saw no woods or redbirds.

Finally, we decided to make an offer, several thousand dollars less than the asking price. We went to McDonald's for lunch, prayed, and called back about the house. The woman accepted our offer, and I felt very stuck with a dismal, dirty old house that was supposed to look white. The rooms were large, but there didn't seem to be enough of them. Once again I thought God had made a mistake.

Back in Prattville we went through the teary good-byes with the dear pastor that had led me to Christ, all of our first Christian family (by this time grown in number to nearly two hundred) and our little farm, and we pulled once again onto the highway. We felt like Abraham, going out not really knowing what lay ahead.

While the moves and constant changes seemed to energize Marvin, they sapped me of energy. Mainly I suffered from being separated from my friends and familiar surroundings. But with his cheerful outlook and boundless energy, Marvin was a great help in getting us settled into this old house.

Our first task was to make the house presentable for Christmas since we moved on the nineteenth of December.

God had not made a mistake. We bought a nine-foot tree and decorated the doors with a few wreaths, and with just the tree lights and a few candles lit, the house looked absolutely regal.

Every moment I was able to appreciate wonderful things about the house I had missed before—like fireplaces in the living room, dining room, and two of the bedrooms. A fireplace is my favorite thing about a house, next to the kitchen. This house had the largest kitchen I had ever seen.

Soon we began getting wallpaper up and flooring down. We closed in the porch and got two large bedrooms and a large entry hall out of that; we opened the attic and got three more bedrooms and a large den.

By the time my decorating juices were running full steam, we had thirteen rooms that we were very proud of and the whole thing, additions and all, cost about fifteen thousand dollars.

We painted the house an autumn gold and the shutters dark green, and all in all it took on an appearance of a poor man's version of "Tara." After everything was in order, it was just perfect for our tastes, pocketbook, and family needs. God had seen to everything.

As we pioneered a successful work among the children of Gadsden, we were extremely happy and assured that we were smack-dab in the center of the Lord's will.

We enjoyed a time when the Lord's hand was clearly on nearly the whole town. Our ministry benefited as churches threw open their doors to help us and for us to help them. They supported us, and we trained teachers to reach lost children. Many were brought to Christ for salvation, and nothing had ever brought us more satisfaction.

We thought we were getting closer and closer to heaven and that nothing could spoil our lives. I had been a Christian a whole three years. I had a lot to learn.

During the Christmas season of 1970 I had the glorious privilege of being invited into seventeen schools to present a visualized Christmas story. All during the last week I had a nagging pain behind my eyes. Since I had a long history of headaches of every sort, I wasn't alarmed; everything else was going well.

Because we were in need of help with the baby and the big house, the Lord brought a dear, tall, black woman into our lives who became Matthew's "Grandma." We could only afford her one or two days a week, and that was at only four dollars a day. Often she would stay for nothing, and Marvin would go to her house to put in a tub or do some other work to better her poor dwelling place, where she cared for her nearly invalid husband. As this dear woman was to go through one of the most trying times of our lives with us, she truly became the hands and eyes of God for me.

Ida had the house sparkling and the baby napping on my last day of teaching. My eyes were tired and aching, and I had to wait for Marvin to come home so he could drive her home—I was afraid to trust my sight. Ida was to have a two-week vacation visiting her son, and what was to take place while she was gone would make it necessary for her to come every day when she returned.

Matthew was just a little over a year old and very playful, but I was not in a playful mood that late afternoon. I begged off from cooking supper, which I rarely ever did, and went to bed. I believed if I rested for a day or so I would soon be functioning again. My folks were coming for Christmas, and I still had baking and some shopping to do. However, my bed rest was to last about four months. I told a doctor friend I thought I had a sinus infection and asked him to give me an antibiotic. He did and somehow I got through Christmas, but I don't remember much about it. I stayed in bed most of the time, and I became increasingly aware that something was very wrong with me. My feet and hands were numb and the left side of my body would sometimes be all numb.

I kept pacifying Mom, Dad, and Marvin, however, by telling them that I was getting better.

The Sunday after Christmas, Mom and Dad were to leave. By this time I was nearly blind. Not wanting to worry them, I casually asked Daddy to cook his own breakfast. When I went to the black and white plaid kitchen to talk to him while he fried his bacon, I fell down for no apparent reason. My left leg just gave way. I laughed off my clumsiness and encouraged my parents on their way—"I'm doing much better."

Later my Mom told me they had had grave doubts about leaving that day, but my stubborn insistence had persuaded them.

Later that Sunday afternoon my bladder refused to function. When the fullness became unbearable, Marvin took me to the emergency room where I was so relieved by the catheterization that I failed to detail the other symptoms, they sounded so foolish. I did briefly mention my dim vision, but I thought it was sinus-related. The emergency room doctor examined my sinuses and ordered me off the medicine. I was relieved, thinking that it was a reaction to the medication that had been making me worse. I was only in the emergency room a couple of hours, then back to my cozy house. The tree was still up and there was much to do, but I just couldn't see well enough to function.

The next day Marvin had a business trip out of town, and he was worried about leaving me; so he asked a friend of ours to stay with me.

She came and brought us our dinner and washed the dishes, and then I said, "Judy, you know Marvin is just a worrywart; I'm fine and I would even be better if you would go home. I feel guilty about taking you away from your family." At my bidding, she left after I promised to call her if I should have a problem. I didn't mean to lie to her. But later that evening I got myself into trouble and had a hard time getting help.

All during the night I kept drinking water to flush out the offending medication. But my bladder at first would only function after running water. Then the later it got, the more stubborn my bladder became, until in the middle of the night I was in immense pain and too embarrassed to call for help. What would I say? The children had been frightened by my dimming eyesight and had camped out on the floor of our giant bedroom.

Before that night was over, I couldn't see the roses on our bedroom wallpaper, and I felt as if I might be dying. I couldn't figure out what could be wrong with me.

When I would get the courage to call someone, I couldn't read the number in the phone book or the numbers on the phone. I didn't want to wake the children and frighten them. If I called a doctor, he would say to come in, and I couldn't. If I called a friend in the middle of the night, I would just feel terrible; so I decided to wait it out.

Finally, after the longest night in my history, 7:00 A.M. arrived. A respectable hour, I thought, in which to ask for help. I had the children call my pastor, who was also a good friend and who would understand that I was too uncomfortable to dress, and would not be too embarrassed to take me to the hospital in my old blue nightgown and winter overcoat.

There were no beds in the emergency room that

morning—not even a cart for me to lie on. So for what seemed like a black eternity, I sat on that chair trying to hold back the tears and be a strong Christian.

The more the pain persisted the less spiritual I felt; in fact I couldn't even think of spiritual things.

Finally, after what seemed like eons, the head nurse borrowed a cot from outside the operating room long enough to catheterize me, but then I had to get back up and sit in that cold hard chair again. I know I must have looked like the ugly stepsister, but I was so blind by that time I didn't care who saw me. I just wanted help from my two towers of strength, "Marvin, where are you?" I cried. "God, where are You?"

When a cart became available I was strapped to it to wait for a bed. I remained on that narrow, hard cart, uncomfortable and cold for the entire day. There is only one word to describe how I felt outside of the discomfort: confused. I just didn't know what was going on.

Once secured on that unyielding cart, I dismissed my pastor, assuring him bravely that I was just fine and that I knew he had many duties other than waiting in an emergency room for one of his parishioners to void with a tube. I didn't say that, of course, but I wasn't really choosing my words too carefully.

When he left, a little of the old nature fear gripped my heart and the enemy of my soul said, "Where are all your Christian friends now? Where is that faith you talk about? I do believe God has deserted you, and here you are all alone. My, my, I feel sorry for you." I hardly knew what to do with these messages, but I needn't have worried. My Father knew just how much I knew about resisting the devil, and He began to fight for me by bringing people into the emergency room to be with me—dear, old seasoned saints who took over praying for me, doctor friends who kept checking on me until I felt totally cared for. Jesus began to speak peace to the storm in my heart. I remembered a verse so precious when I first believed, John 14:27: "Peace, I leave with you; My peace I give unto you; not as the world gives, do I give to you. Let not your heart be troubled, nor let it be fearful." I remember thinking: "Okay, Lord, the time has come for education in new areas of faith—I trust You." As God is my witness, all fear and trouble left me.

The emergency room is not a pleasant place to spend the night, especially if you are blind. I could hear moans and screams. I heard talk of a shooting and rushing nurses and doctors speaking of impending terror in someone's life. But I was not afraid.

I slept fitfully because of the noise. Once when I awakened with a wave of nausea, I was about to call a nurse when I realized someone was near me. I spoke and the voice that answered was male, but I didn't recognize it. I was slightly embarrassed, but God had sent him to hold the pan for me to throw up in.

I found out later he was an elder in the First Presbyterian Church, and he offered to sit many times with me. God provided in so many unusual ways and through so many people it would be impossible to name them.

My dear, blessed Marvin arrived the next day, and while Jesus had spoken peace to my heart, Marvin was like the sun after a storm. He effectually prayed for the room that according to the hospital staff was not to be available for a couple of days. The staff was amazed at the speed with which we moved into one that very day. My husband and I felt much better, but the team of physicians didn't concur.

A neurosurgeon conducted a scanty test in my room that consisted of rubbing me with cotton in different locations, sticking me with a pin, and then doing a spinal tap. After several other tests, one of the doctors told my husband I had the crippler of young adults, multiple sclerosis. My family doctor was not as quick to pin that tag on me and wouldn't put that diagnosis on my chart until I had been to the top neurosurgeons at the University of Alabama Medical Center in Birmingham. There the diagnosis was confirmed.

I knew the Spirit of God was doing something in my life because I was almost constantly filled with a joy unspeakable. I would cry, but they were tears of joy. I didn't understand why I wasn't more upset.

I kept asking people who visited to find the verse that said, ". . . this is my will for you." Finally, Marvin found 1 Thessolanians 5:18: "in every thing give thanks; for this is God's will for you in Christ Jesus." We really believed that the Spirit of God was being released in our lives as we accepted His will, even if it meant permanent blindness and a wheelchair. We had enormous consolation in that belief.

Also of enormous consolation were the multitude of Christians who came to our aid. We had people stuffing money into our hands; one of the local churches set up a medical fund to pay all medical bills; my medication never cost us a dime. Then for four months the wonderful Christian women of our town fixed the most tempting meals, brought them, served them, and cleaned up.

I tried to keep family life as normal as possible and would go to the table to eat.

My family showed their love in so many ways. In fact, it never even dawned on me that Marvin might be repulsed by the way I looked. I didn't know that my pupils stayed dilated or that my eyes bulged in an ugly way. I was pale, and my hair had to have been a mess. I knew that how I looked did not determine how my husband felt about me. I had complete assurance of his love, and for that I will be forever grateful.

When I first got home from the hospital, I smelled ham and other good things, and there was someone busy in my kitchen cleaning the molding leftovers from Christmas out of the refrigerator. It turned out to be the lady who planned and organized the meals that were to come to my family.

That evening a new pastor in town, who had been on the mission field in Africa, came to visit. He said, "You don't even know me, but I have heard a lot about you, and I have a message for you that we send to one another in the field via the radio when someone has fallen seriously ill. 'Brother so and so, God has entrusted Marilee Horton with MS.' "

That was all he said; he prayed with us and left. But that has stayed with me. When something big happens, I try to believe that God sees I'm big enough now to be entrusted with something. As you know by now, I don't always pass the test.

Michael had given me a daily devotional book for Christmas called *Streams in the Desert*, written by Mrs. Charles Cowman. Each day one of my family would read it to me. It was such a comfort.

On February 1, 1971, it said, " 'This thing is from me.' I Kings 12:24." I nearly jumped out of bed. "Read that again," I said.

" 'This thing is from me.' " It went on to say something like this: Have you ever thought of it, that all that concerns you concerns Me too? For ". . . he who touches you, touches the apple of His eye" (Zech. 2:8). It went on telling me that God had sifted this trial through His fingers of love. It wasn't just an accidental tragedy. Rather, it was God's special way of educating me. "You are very precious in My sight" (Isa. 43:4). Let it not be said of me, "But for all this, you did not trust the LORD your God" (Deut. 1:32).

As suggestions that I go to a faith healer came, God's revelation of love confirmed my belief that it would be an insult to God to go to such a person. He had clearly instructed me in His Word that He had allowed this affliction. If I was to be healed, it would be in accordance with James 5:14, "Is anyone among you sick? Let him call for the elders of the church, and let them pray over him, anointing him with oil in the name of the Lord." That being done in obedience, I knew deep in my heart I would be well one day. As a three-year-old Christian, I knew that there is but one mediator between God and man and that is Christ Jesus. I knew that I was as welcome at His throne as anyone, because I was clothed in the righteousness of Jesus Christ Himself.

Testimonies of healings are wonderful, and I never doubt God's ability to heal; but I do know that the testimonies of those who continue praising God and trusting Him when no answer comes have the strength of steel in them. People who have continued to trust despite adversity have inspired millions of troubled hearts. Being blind was not fun, but for me it was temporary. I now have a compassion for blind people that I know I would have never had without that experience.

God met not only my needs during this time but also those of the whole family. Marvin had given up his job in insurance to devote all his time to CEF. We were trusting God for everything and we were not disappointed. A great load was lifted when dear Ida was hired full time for a whole year until I was on my feet again. The money for Ida's salary came every week in cash, and I was never meant to find out who sent it. But one day by accident I found out it was the same dear friend who saw to it (and still does) that this missionary looks like "God is taking care of her." I have had the loveliest clothes to replace the little farm house dresses, clothes that I would have never been able to afford.

As I have spoken and taught in many places in this country, my wardrobe is a constant testimony to God's goodness. The donor would rather die than have me tell who she is. She always pretends she just happens to have all these new clothes in my size, or that she bought them for herself but that the belt doesn't hang right or some other gimpy excuse. She has sewn for my daughter, given us cars, paid for driving lessons, and no telling what all. She has the gift of giving, and God has used her over and over again to encourage us when the tide looked the roughest. Only a great God can repay someone like her.

Marvin had to put up with a lot during my first couple of months home. I had to be taken to and from the urologist every few days to have a catheter replaced. But the ultimate test of devotion was when my husband would remove the tube at home in order to give me a relaxed atmosphere in which I could try to empty my bladder. Each time I would read my Bible, confess every sin I could think of, and then try to believe God for a miracle. I began to make an absolute fetish out of it. It seemed that I was looking for just the right combination—what to read and how much and how to pray. When nothing happened, I blamed myself and felt guilty.

This went on for a couple of months, and then one day while the tube was removed (and I didn't even have the faith to try to see if my bladder would function), I ran a tub full of hot water and got in.

It felt luxurious as I slid down under the billows of suds, and I just started talking to the Lord, "Father, I am sorry, but I can't even work up faith enough to believe that I will ever be normal again. Help Thou my unbelief."

The urge was instant. I still didn't get excited. I dried off and said, "It's okay, Lord, whatever You want." The healing the church elders had prayed for began to manifest itself at that moment.

My heart was full of a truth that God was teaching—that His love is unconditional and there is no proper combination to actuate it.

He is sovereign and I had to see Him as working without dependence on the way I felt or did things. I can see great wisdom in this. If I had hit on a combination, I would have been God-like, and I could have had my own healing meetings, but then who would have gotten the glory?

Since that wonderful time when I surrendered completely to the Lord's will regarding my physical problem, I have never had a moment's trouble with my bladder, in spite of warnings from my urologist, George Walker, that after long-term catheterization I could expect infections. As a Christian he rejoiced as much in the Lord as I did that all was made well by the Great Physician.

I began to strengthen every day. It is almost too boring to go back and detail just when numbness left what part of my body or just when I was able to stop taking steroids and medication for dizziness.

The weekly visits to the doctor for B–12 shots continued for a long time; then visits were monthly, and finally they ended. I don't believe I will be plagued by the MS symptoms again. In fact, I have often wondered if there was a mistake in the original diagnosis, but the doctor said the disease sometimes goes into long remission, so it is too soon to tell if the healing is permanent. The only telltale sign that I know of is the scar tissue on my optic nerve that says that something was wrong, but my vision is perfect now.

I am very careful about what I say about healing. I praise God that I am now well—but I also praise Him for those tough years because we learned more in that valley than on the mountaintops.

NINE

Staging a Suicide

Suicide is not a solitary act, but a vast, expensive production. The cast includes, of course, the "star," but there are many other principal players, as well as bit players and even extras. In a Broadway production the producer rounds up backers to finance the show. In staging a suicide this is not true. The producer gets his cast together, chooses the right time, rehearses the script carefully with the star, gives last minute instructions, and then waits for the results.

Keep in mind that in staging a suicide a successful run would be only a one shot thing. The producer goes his merry way and leaves the poor cast and crew to pick up the pieces and pay the bills.

I believe the producer of a suicide is *always* Satan.

There are many excuses that people give as reasons for suicidal thinking, but unless a person is severely mentally ill, events leading up to what I call "staging" are usually *cumulative*, and it takes considerable staging to effect a suicide.

1. *Illness and pain.* I wonder if we have even thought through how we might react to serious illness or pain? I am aware that God's grace to endure such is not available until needed, but shouldn't we bolster up weak areas in our fortress against the

attacker of the body? Of course, we are to rejoice in all things, but just what if the pain is long and severe? If the master of deceit has his way, tiny seeds of bitterness begin to sprout and send out little shoots, expelling the poison of self-pity. The star is now ready for a proposal from the producer. God is indeed sufficient, but we must draw upon that sufficiency.

2. *Circumstances disrupted.* The pleasant things in our lives are entirely welcome to stay forever. In fact we are terribly disturbed when our comforts and pleasures are interrupted. For example, when Sylvia, my best friend and confidant, moved several hundred miles away, I tried to see it from God's point of view; I had placed almost too much importance on her, depending on her sometimes instead of the Lord. I believed that God would teach me to call Him my best friend, but it was painful and I wasn't prepared for the type of grief that rocked my being. My friend's moving away was like losing a loved one in death. As the shock takes over, the producer says, "You have let that God of yours be your manager and you see what a fix you're in. He doesn't really want to make you happy. I can offer you a much better deal."

3. *Circumstances remain the same.* Just as there are circumstances that we want unchanged, there are those in each life that we would have altered. Why is it those that always seem so stable? "Why didn't my pain go away instead of my friend?" A childish question? Yes, but we know that there is still that little child in each one of us that wants answers.

Despair and despondency can attach themselves like bloodsuckers when you live day after day, year after dreary year with an alcoholic or an invalid. Your mind becomes open to suggestions. The liar says, "You need a little relief, a little change in scenery. Why not read that risqué novel or go to that latest R-rated movie—you need a little adventure!" Satan loves to get us to give in to his ideas, and he plants little pictures in our memory banks that we can never erase. Just one dirty movie or one pornographic book can allow him to set up a small army in your mind that shoots darts from within instead of without.

4. *Disappointment.* Things don't always go according to your plans. In my case I had planned for years before I ever married that I would marry a stable man like my daddy, one who would stay at the same job for thirty years and come home at the same time every day and read the paper. Of course, he would be more interesting than that, but that was the framework of my fairy tale. When my mate took a job traveling, Satan sent little computer cards to my data bank: "He is choosing to be away from home. You have failed to make home attractive enough for him to want to be here."

If you receive those data cards, you had better fold, spindle, or mutilate. If you don't, a certain resignation to unhappiness crowns King Defeat. From defeat it seems all downhill.

If you don't refuse the spirit of heaviness and discouragement early, it will be increasingly hard to do so. Everyday dreariness begins to loom large, and you overreact. "I can't go out; it is too much effort to dress. Oh, will I ever get this house clean, or get the laundry put away?" Each tiny fact of life takes on super-large proportions, and you don't feel like doing anything. There is (in your mind) no purpose anymore, no one even cares anymore. . . .

TA DA!—CURTAIN UP—DRUM ROLL.

Enter Satan (in a condescending tone): "I could have told you it wouldn't work; Jesus Christ was just another crutch like your booze, but now you have dropped the crutch. You are no better than you were before, only older and a little more foolish. You want to help your family? GET OUT OF THEIR LIVES!"

Add a bit of depressing music in the background, and the scene is set: unmade beds, dirty dishes, dusty furniture, dirty clothes piled around.

The star (rallying for the moment): "Satan, I resist you in the name of the Lord Jesus Christ."

Satan: "Okay for now, but I will be back. I'm sure sorry you have been in so much pain; too bad your God has forgotten you."

Exit Satan, laughing.

The star: "Forgotten?"

Unfortunately these productions are being staged in thousands of homes. Just as a Broadway show can close early if not successful, so this production can be stopped by early resistance to Satan.

Just as the main character was left questioning God in the above, there are children of God in varying stages of rehearsal for staging a suicide. It must be stopped.

Maybe you are just slightly giving in to self-pity and discouragement. I beg you, find out who is controlling your life before the climactic ending, which will leave your family and friends to pick up the pieces in confusion.

I don't pretend to know all the answers, but I directly connect Satan to the ever-increasing number of Christians attempting suicide. I think if we seek to uncover just who would profit most by an act of self-destruction on the part of a Christian, we will see that regardless of what caused the person to be cast down, suicidal thinking is satanic.

In contrast to what Paul said to the Corinthians in his second letter—"in order that no advantage be taken of us by Satan; for we are not ignorant of his schemes" (2:11)—I believe many Christians *are ignorant* of his schemes. I believe the Bible bears out, as well as human history, that just at the peak and prime of a Christian's life and service, just when he is the most effective, it becomes the purpose of the enemy of our soul to snuff us out. His three favorite areas are scandal, apostasy, and suicide. What better way to hurl a slap in the face of God than to have a "successful" Christian snuff himself out?

Ephesians 6:12 is clear about the invisible war that has been raging round about us since the fall of Lucifer: "For we wrestle not against flesh and blood, but against principalities, against powers, against the rulers of the darkness of this world, against spiritual wickedness in high places" (KJV). Could this passage be any more emphatic about who it is we are fighting?

The world has been compared to a stage on which a great drama is being played. It has also been compared to a battlefield. The fight is on right now for the souls and lives of men and women. That the foe is invisible does not diminish his power; nor does the fact that he is clearly defeated through the death and resurrection of the Lord Jesus Christ slow down his efforts to enlist us in his army.

Prior to my suicide attempt I had a tremendous appetite for the Word of God. I loved prophecy and the great doctrines that are so precious. I had grown in the grace and knowledge of the Lord Jesus in the eight years that I had been saved, and I loved teaching and serving the Lord. But I had not educated myself on the tactics of the enemy.

"Don't dwell on Satan," I was told. I now know there is a difference between dwelling on and being sensibly knowledgeable about Satan.

We are taught to sing "I am a Soldier of the Cross," "The Fight Is On," and "Onward Christian Soldiers." But, unfortunately, unlike a soldier in an earthly battle who is drilled in defensive weaponry, I failed to pinpoint on the map of my mind the areas of weakness where the enemy might strike. I failed to let God pull down strongholds that Satan was building, as I opened the door of self-pity and inadvertently gave Satan entrance. It was *my duty* to "put on the whole armor of God." But evidently there was a "hole" in the "whole" because I was not able to stand "against the schemes of the devil" (Eph. 6:11).

I am not a kook looking under every rock and behind every bush for a demon. Neither do I quake and quiver, fearfully waiting to see what the devil will do to me next. All of this I attribute to the fact that I am eternally happily secure in the Lord Jesus Christ. How vital that is.

However, I do not negate the power and the craftiness of the prince of this world and the ruler of darkness as he tries to smear my testimony. And, I certainly don't believe his con job of trying to make himself just a joke by cheerfully hiding his true personality behind a red suit with a tail.

In searching for the answers to the question I know you are asking, "What would make a real child of God try to destroy herself?" "Why wasn't God sufficient enough to prevent a self-inflicted death," I explored every avenue and read many books. A book that is an invaluable tool to the Christian is *What Demons Can Do to Saints,* by Merrill F. Unger. Another book that has been beneficial to me is *Happiness Is a Choice*, by Frank A. Minirth, M.D. and Paul D. Meier, M.D.

Unger's book deals with the power of Satan and his demons and ways he afflicts Christians. *Happiness Is a Choice* reveals that often we are our own enemy in choosing to believe that we must live depressed, defeated, and despairing lives.

I was aware almost immediately after I became lucid in the hospital that Satan was the one I was dealing with. But, as I asked myself, "How did he gain such control?" I honestly didn't know the answer. All I knew was that Satan apparently wanted to destroy me, and he had duped me into believing his lie that my life was to be lived out defeated. He talked me into believing I was a flop and that my family would be better off without me.

As I began to dig into God's Word for answers to my questions, I saw some definite doors that I had left ajar in my life. That was how Satan gained entrance.

1. The first door was a *poor self-image*. In choosing for myself a perfectionist standard, I had set unbe-

lieveably high goals that could never be reached. That always led to disappointment and discouragement. I drove myself in every area of life and was merciless on myself when I failed to reach the impossible goals. "The Impossible Dream" could have been my theme song, as I was driven by my own unconscious motives and conflicts. Satan wasn't actually responsible for that; I was. I failed to realize that I was "fearfully and wonderfully made" (Ps. 139:14). I failed to believe, "I can do all things through Him . . ." (Phil. 4:13). As I strived in my own self-effort to be approved by God, I pushed open a door just in time to let Satan's friends get their foot in.

Psychologists have spent considerable time finding and naming the many causes of depression that are crippling a large percentage of the world's population. Several good biblical books have been written on the subject as it relates to Christians. Two of these that prove most helpful are: *Spiritual Depression* by Martyn Lloyd-Jones and *How To Win Over Depression* by Tim LaHaye. Thus, it is not my purpose here to dwell on that which is ably covered by these good works. I recommend that every Christian read books such as these even if you are not plagued with depression. We all know someone who is, and it would offer us a little deeper understanding.

The worst possible thing to say to a depressed person is, "Don't be depressed." Who in the world chooses to "be depressed"? And if a person did, once they experienced the real pain that is depression, they would certainly want out of the deep, black hole. I can't believe anyone wants to sit in a chair for hours on end, staring into space without any hope. It does *no* good to tell a person in this bleak, unproductive, morose frame of mind to "pull yourself up by your bootstraps." A deeply depressed person has lost sight of even his bootstraps.

Some of the causes of depression I have observed most often have been the loss of a loved one, bitterness, financial setbacks, unsaved family members, and in my own case, physical illness and pain. Usually in all these cases there was a general weariness with the circumstance. This led to door number two.

2. *Anger.* When I honestly evaluated, with the help of a Christian counselor and psychologist, what could have caused me to sink to the depths that Psalms 102 speaks of, there was a need to admit the deep-seated anger I felt against God for my circumstances. I didn't mind admitting that I was frustrated; most Christians will go that far. But we wince at being faced with our own self-pity. And even deeper than that, behind the "sweet little Christian" facade that most of us have been trained to keep up, we see our anger, not just at the people we blame and the situations we blame, but at God. According to Ephesians 4:26,27, anger opens the door to Satan. Do we refuse to see the sovereign God? 1 Kings 12:24 reads in part, ". . . this thing has come from Me."

Is He only answering our prayer? Did we ask Him to conform us to the image of Christ? Are these things necessary to educate us? How many times I cried, "Stop, Lord, I didn't know it would hurt so."

It was not that way at first. No, I was very patient with God in the beginning. For that couple of years when I experienced real physical affliction in the form of multiple sclerosis, I could see God in it all. I could praise Him and believe He would cause the flowers of His grace to bloom in the darkness.

I believe there must be a difference in the way a Christian suffers. We must behave differently at the hospital; we must radiate joy.

I did these things, but there came a moment when a tiny thought flashed through my mind, *Enough is enough.*

I can't remember when that thought came, but when it did the stage was set, the producer was watching and listening and when that barrier was down, he was free to set up his strongholds. I can almost hear him saying, "All right gang, the time is here. She is giving in to vain imaginations; she has stopped seeing the good that is working in her life; let's set up more strongholds. Fear, get moving; Doubt, start building; Pity, take over; Discouragement, you have a good foothold, keep building."

So the invisible army began to play fiery dart games with me in the form of negative thoughts. "You sure are a disappointment to your family. You have really let God down. You are going to be a hopeless cripple, sick and in pain all your life. You are useless and in everyone's way."

I was ill-prepared for this onslaught, after I had been victorious for so long. But before long I became an active participant. Instead of applying James 4:7 ". . . resist the devil and he will flee from you," I began to harbor and nurture these thoughts, *Satan's thoughts*. It is easy to quote James 4:7, but just how would you instruct someone to resist? I had the verses quoted to me, but it was the "how" that I needed.

There are many biblical cases of depression and suicidal thinking and it is quite interesting that while this is wrong, some of these people were men after God's heart. They were not "washouts"; they were men used mightily of God, before and even after their trip to the "slough of despond." Let's take a look at a few of them:

Moses—Numbers 11:14,15: "I alone am not able to carry all this people, because it is too burdensome for me. So if Thou art going to deal thus with me, please kill me at once. . . ." (He was weary of serving the Lord.)

Job—Job 7:15,16: "So that my soul would choose suffocation, death rather than my pains. I waste away; I will not live forever; leave me alone; for my days are but a breath." Job 7:20: ". . . I am a burden to myself." I can't say enough about that last statement; it is one thing to be a burden to family and even society, but being a burden to yourself is a miserable feeling.

Jonah—Jonah 4:3: "Therefore now, O LORD, please take my life from me, for death is better to me than life." (He was out of fellowship, disobedient, perplexed, and fainting.)

David penned many of the Psalms that minister to our aching hearts; these came not from inner poetry but from inner agony.

Even our hero from the New Testament, *Paul*, "despaired even of life" after being "burdened excessively" (2 Cor. 1:8). But I believe Paul, who penned the Scriptures that deal with our battle with

Satan, was thoroughly furnished for warfare, and he did not sink into the purple pit of self-pity and suicidal thoughts.

If I had to vote for someone I thought had a right to give up life, it would be Job. I doubt that anyone, anywhere had more to contend with. But he continued to bless God and in the end God blessed him.

The man I most strongly identified with and who ministered the most to me when I was trusting the Lord to provide my own private "brook" was Elijah in 1 Kings 17–19.

Elijah did not become depressed and suicidal over testings. He was sent to hide himself after a dramatic public ministry. I don't think he relished living a life of seclusion by a brook that had lost its babble and being fed each day by a catering service that did not have a triple "A" rating. But he could cope with it, and so can most Christians cope with hardships and testings.

The Word does not indicate that Elijah got the blues over what was done to his self-image when God sent him to seemingly mooch off a poor widow woman, either. No identity crisis here!

I don't see him eaten up with guilt feelings over having to ask help not only from a Gentile in a heathen city but from a woman no less. He just allowed God to provide, and in so doing the widow and her son were provided for too.

Elijah's complete obedience this far was followed by more testing. The widow had one son and he died. She blamed Elijah. Did he request death for this false accusation? No. He didn't run for the pill bottle; he was not a morbid, self-destructive escapist.

In 1 Kings 18:22 Elijah indulges in the only self-pity that I see in his life. For Elijah and so many others the key word is "alone." Was he alone? No, and neither are any of Christ's blood-bought saints. That is a lie from the devil. The next chapter indicates that he nurtured the thought (see 1 Kings 19:10) because he brought it up to the Lord. It was one negative thought—just one block in the stronghold—but it was something to build on. Do you feel all ALONE?

Is it possible to continue on in a powerful service and still harbor a negative thought? Yes, for a while. Elijah's stunning victory on Mount Carmel indicates that he had not lost the power of God. But Elijah came down with a supreme case of the jitters and very nearly cried out, "Bury me under the juniper tree" in 19:4. It reads: "But he himself went a day's journey into the wilderness, and came and sat down under a juniper tree; and he requested for himself that he might die; and said, 'It is enough; now O LORD, take away my life. . . .' "

I don't believe Elijah was frightened by Jezebel. I believe he heard Satan as a "roaring lion" growl at him through Jezebel when she said, "I'm going to get you." I am sure that is what I heard—roars and deep growls—in the spring of 1975 as I sat under my own personal juniper tree. I succumbed to fear, not knowing I had the weapon to resist Satan right in my hands.

Had I been prepared for such an attack, I would have known how to take the weapon, His Word, and use it with authority, saying, "Satan, God hath not given us the spirit of fear; but of power, and of love, and of a sound mind (2 Tim. 1:7, KJV). In the name of

Jesus Christ, flee from me." The only weapon is the Word, and we must bolster our weak points with appropriate verses.

God was plenteous in mercy to Elijah in 1 Kings 19:5–7. He was also gracious to show love and most of all forgiveness to me during that "dark night of the soul." Thanks to His mercy, I am once again well; the smile that I thought was gone forever has returned, and I am excited about life. But all of this didn't happen overnight.

I wonder if we realize what God would have us do for those who are going through personal agony. Angels ministered food and drink and rest to Elijah.

Did God send His angels to me? I think he did, in the form of my Christian brothers and sisters who ministered to me in many ways. My neglect of food and rest had affected my mind, body, and nerves. Friends helped with the children so I could rest; others brought tempting foods to encourage my lazy palate. Many just touched my hand or hugged me and said, "We love you and it's all right." My friends didn't understand, but they didn't judge. They just tried to help me through it, and I can never thank them enough.

In turn, I now try to give aid and comfort to others who are suffering. It is important for us to let God use us to help make someone well. It is equally important for the one suffering not to discourage those whom God chooses to use to minister to us when we need a touch from Him.

3. *Drugs.* This third door ajar in my life was surprising even to me, and disgusting. It is the hardest for me to admit, but if it was so easy for me to get in

that position I wonder how many others are there right now? Drug addiction. Sounds awful doesn't it? Especially coming from a Christian.

Now it is hard for me to realize I was so blind and stupid. In trying to gain necessary information about Satan for my Bible classes, I kept running across the word "sorcery" in my Bible. Verses like Isaiah 47:9,12 troubled me. I saw the word "witchcraft" in Galatians 5:20 (KJV) and discovered that it could be translated "sorcery." It was listed as a work of the flesh. I always attributed sorcery to magicians and witches and certainly thought that was one sin no one could lay to my account. But then I looked up the word in Vine's Expository Dictionary of New Testament Words.

> Sorcery—noun—PARMAKIA (or EIA) (Eng., Pharmacy, etc.) primarily signified the use of medicine, drugs, spells; then poisoning; then sorcery.
> In sorcery, the use of drugs, whether simple or potent was generally accompanied by incantations and appeals to occult powers, . . . designed to keep the applicant or patient from the attention and power of demons, but actually to impress the applicant with the mysterious resources and powers of the sorcerer.

My mind immediately jumped to the sleeping pills. Was that drug actually an open door for demon activity? I had even thanked God for providing a safe and nonaddicting way for me to get to sleep when I was having trouble.

Was it really an open door? Yes, I believe it was. Let me explain.

At first it was innocent enough, and maybe for

most people it wouldn't have caused any trouble. But, Satan, knowing that I had been an escapist in the past through alcohol, picked up on the opportunity to get at me with the first prescription.

The first prescription was written in good conscience during my many months of staying all day and night in bed with MS symptoms.

My complaint was, "After constant bed rest I just can't get to sleep at night." Thus a prescription was written by a dear, compassionate physician who was not at all aware of my weakness or Satan's tricks.

I must admit that with my very first pill I loved the euphoric feeling and the lack of struggle to relax and get to sleep.

After I began to improve and be active again, I found that my old routine, with its pressures and time commitments, was improved by being able to take a pill when I decided to go to bed. I would get right to sleep in fifteen minutes without a struggle.

As time went on, I could always get a prescription if I used the excuse that I was going to be traveling and I couldn't sleep well away from home. That was true, but before long I was using sleeping pills nearly every night. So far as I knew my heart at that point, I didn't believe I was abusing the medication. I was just taking one capsule at night.

In 1974 when I began to have horrible, long-lasting headaches, it seemed that when a pain medication wouldn't help I could take a sleeping pill and at least get an hour or so of rest. I always woke up with the headache, and I wonder now if the pills themselves were the culprit.

I began to look forward to the small period of time

when I would be under the influence of the pill. As I ran from doctor to doctor to find the cause of the horrendous headaches, I would mention my sleeplessness to each as if he were the first and would secure yet another prescription. So, little by little, the "sorcery" was taking over, and I didn't even know it.

I always had a large supply of pills, and I am quite ashamed now of my ways of conning the doctors. I marvel at how easy it is and wonder how many people are doing the same thing. I would have been adamant in my defense in this matter. In fact, I was quite a crusader against drug and alcohol abuse.

I didn't actually look up the word "addict" until this writing because I knew what it meant, or so I thought. According to Webster, an addict is one who devotes or surrenders oneself to something habitually or excessively.

My pill taking was becoming a habit, though not an actual physical hunger, and it was becoming excessive. My devotion to Jesus Christ and His service began to slide backward, and pills were on my mind too much of the time. Little did I know that I should have been looking out for the "wiles" or trickery of the devil as mentioned in Ephesians 6:11.

Here's a little test to see if you are an addict: What are you surrendered and devoted to?

Late in 1974 depression became my middle name. After undergoing horrible tests to determine the cause of my headaches, I was convinced I would never be well or free from pain again.

During this time I began to undergo a drastic personality change, which I believe was a result of being put on the drug thorazine. I would just drag, like a zombie, through day after day. About the only excitement I had at that time was taking a sleeping pill and having about fifteen minutes of euphoria (not an hour any longer but fifteen minutes). Then I began taking two or three pills at a time because one didn't do the job.

I wrote to the neurosurgeon who had put me on thorazine and asked if the drug could cause depression. In his reply he told me it is sometimes used to treat depression. I have learned since then that thorazine is a very potent mood-altering drug, which can indeed be used to treat severely depressed persons but which can also have adverse effects on certain individuals.

Any time family members questioned my use of pills, I justified myself by saying the pills were not addictive and that I had to have some relief if I was not to be in pain continually.

I was confusing physical addiction with psychological addiction. My body did not crave the drug, but psychologically I looked for every opportunity to escape the hell I was beginning to inhabit in my own mind.

During February and March of 1975 I became so desperate for relief from pain and fear that on many days after the children went to school I would take one or two pills, go upstairs to Mike's windowless room, where I couldn't hear the doorbell or telephone, cover my head with a pillow, and have fifteen minutes of what I thought was peace. Afterwards I would be nauseous the rest of the day. How blind I was.

I can see now how Satan had disguised himself as

an "angel of light." He promised me relief through the use of drugs, or sorcery, when it seemed all else had failed. I was playing into his hands, believing a lie. My true peace was missing because I was worshiping at the shrine of my idol—the sleeping pill. First John 5:21 says, "Little children, guard yourselves from idols." He began to use the same trick on me as he used on Eve in the garden, "God doesn't really love you." As she had believed so did I, and we both disobeyed and got into trouble.

As I began discovering Satan's use of drugs in tricking God's children, I was able to see why the power in my bathroom was so strong when I heard, "Mrs. FAILURE, take all the pills." Little wonder I couldn't resist. I should have resisted much earlier. He had gained a foothold with the first pill, and then he inched his way in month after month. He was in no hurry; he took his time convincing me that the drugs were necessary, and even a wonderful gift from God.

After the suicide attempt I came home to a full bottle of pills hidden in a drawer. And believe it or not I used them. I still didn't recognize that Satan was actually using the pills. I knew he was feeding me with self-destructive thoughts, but I didn't credit him with enough intelligence to actually plan my self-destructive habits. I fought off the thoughts nearly every moment, and I stopped taking the pills in the daytime. But every day I wanted to. Of course, my supply was limited, and I became more careful about saving them.

Three months after the suicide attempt, we moved to Florida where the battle for my mind and body became as fierce as it ever was. It was only through the trust that I placed in my dear Christian doctor, Bill Faust, and our Savior that I gained the deliverance I now enjoy.

When I ran out of the Alabama supply of sleeping pills, I called Bill and told him I couldn't sleep and needed a prescription. He wrote one prescription for a sleeping pill as weak to me as aspirin, and when I complained he let me know firmly that I couldn't have more of any kind.

I was angry with him, and I felt guilty because I knew he had seen through me. He put me on an antidepressant and one tranquilizer at bedtime, and much to my joy I was able to sleep almost normally.

As I began to get victory over my self-destructive thoughts, I began to get well and even felt that taking any medication was a sin. I withdrew from the antidepressant and tranquilizer. After a few nights of sleeplessness and a giant headache, I went back to the doctor and told him of my self-prescribed actions. I am sure he had just about had it with me before I was able to trust him, not only as a Christian brother but also as the physician God wanted me to place myself under. So I trusted him and I went back on an antidepressant and a tranquilizer at bedtime. I began to sleep well, function normally, and be productive.

One day when I called to have the prescriptions refilled, my doctor said, "Marilee, I'm going to take you off the tranquilizer." I panicked and just knew I couldn't sleep without it, but the Lord impressed me to trust Him to work through Dr. Faust. Much to my surprise I have slept fine and have not had a tranquilizer in over two years.

Once again I was plagued by doubts as to whether I needed to take an antidepressant. Bill explained that he honestly believes I have a chemical imbalance that causes the depression to some extent. He said I was functioning so well with just the one medication that I should continue taking it until he decided otherwise. I almost laughed when I realized that once Satan lost the war over my taking too many drugs, he now wanted me to feel guilty about taking the one I really needed.

I almost hesitated to be completely honest here, because I know that many of you well-meaning friends will be quick to say, "She shouldn't take anything!" Don't say it. I have been all through that, and the Lord has revealed something to me as I have counseled with many women. Not all causes of depression and insomnia are evil. There are people who suffer from hypoglycemia, who if not treated properly suffer such deep depressions that it often leads to suicide. Correcting such chemical imbalances is not a sin. If you are a diabetic you take insulin. That is a chemical imbalance—corrected.

You may be experiencing a period of depression just now or know someone who is. Let me urge you not to wait too long before seeking help. Following are some suggested steps to take:

1. Make a list and honestly name what it is that is bothering you—fear, what kind; anger, at whom; bitterness; discouragement, etc. Share your list and feelings with a trusted physician or counselor.

2. Spread out all your needs before the Lord, go to the Word, and then ask God to reveal if you are out of His will. Be willing to confess any sin He reveals and

return to the place of blessing. It has probably taken a while to get where you are, so don't expect overnight relief, but remember God delights to educate the "apple of His eye."

3. Be sure the enemy has not led you into false teaching by suggesting that something be added to the gospel of grace. Remember your Christian life is based on fact and not feeling. Be careful of getting lured into groups that promise something "full" or "everything Jesus wants you to have." Jesus *is* everything. In Him and in you dwell the fullness of the Godhead.

4. Memorize 2 Corinthians 10:4,5 and Isaiah 26:3. Practice mental gymnastics. Literally take your mind off negative things and put it on Jesus Christ and the empty tomb and all that the Resurrection signifies. Second Corinthians 10:5 mentions "taking every thought captive to the obedience to Christ." Do you realize that you can only concentrate on one thought at a time? It may seem like hundreds are crowding into your mind, but you have to choose which one to concentrate on. Be careful how you choose.

5. If you are still not enjoying peace of mind, but are fearful, anxious, and despairing, you may need to seek counseling. Many pastors are well trained in this, and of course their desire is to help you become victorious. There are Christian counseling centers in many areas of the country, and now there seems to be an increase in the number of Christian psychiatrists.

I am well aware of the many well-meaning Christians who will advise against these steps; I think I have heard them all. I didn't even know myself, until it was nearly too late, just how serious it is to fool around with the demon depression. Before the Lord, this is something you must decide. Ask the Lord to open and close doors for you.

If you have had thoughts of suicide, please take them seriously and deal with them. Even after I was seemingly "out of the woods," Satan would bombard me with suicidal thoughts; finally one day the Lord showed me a very simple weapon for that and it worked. I simply said, "Satan, these thoughts are not from God, neither are they mine—they are yours and I reject them on the grounds that Jesus said, 'I came that they might have life, and might have it abundantly' [John 10:10]. Now I want to live, so in the name of the Lord Jesus Christ—you leave me alone!" PRAISE GOD I am free!

I know that I am not immune to evil thoughts, but from that day until this I have not had even one self-destructive thought, to the praise and honor of Jesus Christ. Do I have down days? Of course, but as I "put on a mantle of praise instead of a spirit of fainting" (Isa. 61:3), the old juniper tree fades into the distance.

NOTE: Understanding depression, its causes and the cure, has never been an easy thing. Now, however with a book like *Happiness Is a Choice*, by Frank B. Minirth, M.D., and Paul D. Meier, M.D., a lay person can at least have some concept of what is happening to him and what the choices are. The kind of medications used are listed with their effects. Biblical principles are used throughout. I believe this book is a significant contribution to Christians who, contrary to much thought, are just as prone to depression as a non-Christian if the circumstances are right.

TEN

You Shall Not Die

This is the day,
  this is the day
That the Lord hath made,
  that the Lord hath made.
We will rejoice,
  we will rejoice
And be glad in it,
  and be glad in it.

This was the Scripture chorus I awoke with one morning three years after my suicide attempt.

As I lay, fully rested, in my four-poster bed waiting for the second alarm to go off, I was unusually filled with joy as I sang the chorus over and over.

I was puzzled by this overwhelming happiness, since I hadn't gotten to bed before 2:30 A.M. for the two previous nights. Then I remembered the Bible class I was teaching on how to claim the filling of the Spirit by faith.

We were learning about the fruits of the Spirit. Love, joy, and peace were certainly evident in my life on this morning, and it would be easy to teach that these were gifts from God.

Later that morning, while hanging clothes on the line, the sun was embracing my arms and back and

133

crowning the top of my head, and the birds were chirping their happy messages to one another, or maybe they were praising God.

An easy gentle breeze moved the sheets I was hanging towards me, and with that breeze the most delicious fragrance this side of glory brushed my nostrils. I was almost overcome with the sweetness of the orange blossoms on the six trees in our backyard.

I left my wicker clothes basket, walked across the fresh, dew-covered lawn, and buried my face in the tender, white blossoms. I was struck at the same moment with what day it was—March 30.

With my face buried in one of God's beautiful creations and with my feet on His warm earth, I worshiped, saying, "Thank You, Lord, for bringing me to this place in my life, where I am happy and content just to be alive.

"Thank You for birthing purpose and meaning out of the blackest hours of my life.

"Thank You that I can smell this gorgeous fragrance when just three years ago all I could smell was death.

"Thank You that I have the strength to hang out clothes.

"Thank You for healthy children who have faded out all that denim on the line.

"Thank You for the husband who helps me wear the daisies off both sides of those sheets.

"Thank You that I didn't leave my side of our bed vacant.

"Most of all, thank You for Jesus Christ and for loving and forgiving me.

"Oh, God of the Universe, I worship and adore You!"

If a neighbor happened to be looking on they would probably have had grave doubts about the fact that I was in better mental condition than ever before. But I was.

On the same date *just three years earlier,* like Jonah, in bitterness and self-pity over my lot in life, I had found it impossible to go on. The feelings of impossibility had come from the enemy, for the Lord says, "For nothing will be impossible with God" (Luke 1:37).

I began to ask myself the same questions I had considered three years earlier. Why didn't I die? Why did God give me another chance when so many others were not given that chance? Why was the very first verse that came lucidly to my drugged mind during those first days: "And as for you, you meant evil against me, but God meant it for good to bring about this present result, to preserve many people alive" (Gen. 50:20).

Was it possible that we were in the land of sunshine and orange blossoms for the express purpose of "preserving many people alive"? Just then I recalled a telephone conversation I had had the evening before with a depressed, suicidal woman, and I knew the answer was yes! She had said, "Just looking into your face when you talk to me calms me. When I look at your vibrant life, I know God can do that for me too."

She was just one of many the Lord of comfort has allowed me to share with in this city that I thought was too big for a small town girl.

Lest you think my arrival at this state of contentment came without a struggle, permit me to dispel that notion.

The excitement that always swelled in our family each summer as we made our long trek to Florida for vacation was hatefully absent that early March of 1975 when Marvin and I went to Tampa for a job interview.

I never considered living in Florida when I sang, "Anywhere with Jesus I will gladly go." Florida was just for fun in the sun, not a serious place to live.

I was in such a state of depression when the committee issued us that call in February that I neither fought Marvin's usual zeal for new adventure nor did I share it. I was in the strange position of having my body moving while inwardly I was standing still. Everything went on around me as normal; I could even put a plastic smile on my ruby red lips and say what I knew was expected of me, but all real living had ceased for me.

When I visited my parents who were vacationing not far from Tampa, they noticed my gauntness, my unusual calmness, and my eyes made blank by the drug that had reduced me to a haggard robot.

Since the committee had never seen me before, they had no way of knowing there was anything wrong with me—that in two short weeks I would try to end my stay on this earth.

I heard Marvin telling the committee that night in March of all the great plans he had, since we would have the challenge of a large, urban area such as Tampa. I vaguely remember hearing him say, "If you will have us, we believe the Lord would have us come." I continued to pick at my Greek salad not really aware that these ponderous plans would include me.

I smiled sweetly as an offer of a house (badly in need of repairs) was made, and we went to look at it in the pitch black with only a flashlight. I had always said I could be content in a cave; I would just put out a tablecloth, some flowers, and some curtains and it would be home. With this house, I saw the falseness of that theory. It was incredibly ugly.

One room we went in had been used for storage of motorcycles, paint cans, and other such items, and I heard Marvin say, "We could make a den here." I shuddered in the damp blackness and said, "That would be fine."

When we returned to Alabama the next day, I somehow never really thought we would move or that I would ever have to live in that house.

I don't remember being overwhelmed with suicidal thoughts before this time, but I was so deeply depressed that I was not coping with reality (partly as a result of thorazine). And within two weeks I was a crushed heap in Satan's hands.

While coming out of that dark sleep in 1975, I didn't think past whatever moment it was. But as I began to strengthen I realized that we had actually said we would move to Tampa, and all the wheels were in motion for a move the end of June.

The children had already been enrolled in a Christian school for the next year. It seemed too late to back out, and I just had to trust Marvin's decision and direction from the Lord.

After an all too brief three-month recuperation, we

had packed all our dear memories in our hearts and all of our material goods in cardboard boxes, and the place that was once just a pleasant vacation spot to us became our final destination.

It was almost humorous—the signs that bedecked the Florida interstate highway. They began just across the state line: "Visit Africa." "Visit Busch Gardens in Tampa." Mile after mile I was faced with pictures of elephants, tigers, tropical plants, and "Visit Africa." It wasn't the least bit humorous to me. My life had been resurrected by my Lord and His physicians, but I wondered, "Why did they let my sense of humor die? I could almost always find something to laugh about before."

The transition from thirteen large, rambling rooms into five-and-one-half tiny, chopped-up rooms that to me had *no* possibilities of ever being home or even comfortable was extremely distasteful in my condition. I am always ashamed of my attitude of ungratefulness over that house, but I have chosen to be totally honest so you would see one more wart on me.

The couple who offered it to us to use, rent-free, until we could find a suitable home were most generous; they knew the house was in a state of disrepair and did much to make it livable before we moved. I am very thankful for their graciousness to me. I must have come across as a very selfish, spoiled brat, constantly complaining about the house, the heat, the horrible bugs, and the hideous sand that was to become a part of our life.

All I wanted to do was jump on any vehicle heading north and go home. I literally hated everything about the move and thought I was being punished for my sins. My erroneous view of God was showing.

To add to this new despair was the fact that six weeks after moving we would experience the first drafty space in our nest as Michael would go back to Birmingham to fulfill his dream. He had won a full scholarship on the basis of his tremendous tenor voice and was excited about studying with a very credible voice teacher.

After the moving day, I began to muddle through the horror of trying to get my life going again against, for me, the worst odds in history. I was confused because in the hospital I had been brighter, more hopeful for a full recovery.

Even before moving, amid all the farewell parties and visits by the friends that had bejeweled my life like a great crown, I had felt as though I were on the road to recovery. I was on antidepressant medication, but that July I knew I wasn't over the hump yet, and the positive feelings that I would be well again began to disintegrate. Satan still had his foot in the door.

I would look at Michael across the dinner table and burst into tears, knowing that part of my life was dying and that he was just the first of four who would leave the nest that I had woven too tightly around them. *Dread* and *panic* took up their old posts, and while I didn't exactly welcome them, I was comfortable with them.

I had grave questions as to whether I would ever be capable of doing what we came to do—train teachers in methods of teaching children the Bible. I was afraid I wouldn't remember the lessons; afraid of new people; afraid they would expect too much; afraid of the big city.

"How will I ever tackle this city with no sense of direction?" It was a big joke to all who knew me that I couldn't find my way out of a paper bag. I had forgotten the verse that had been very important to me once: "For God hath not given us the spirit of fear; but of power, and of love, and of a sound mind" (2 Tim. 1:7, KJV). For some reason still unclear to me, I had not learned my lesson, and I was again allowing the enemy to trouble me.

I began learning again in the agonizing August heat when we were preparing for Michael's departure. It was then that the Lord began to teach me the truth of offensive and defensive weaponry against the enemy.

I had read that I should find appropriate verses for each situation and jab them into the heart of the disturber of peace. I tried it; every time I would get emotional about the impending vacancy, I would say (aloud if possible): "Satan, it is written, 'Thou wilt keep him in perfect peace whose mind is stayed on thee, because he trusteth in thee!' Now, you flee from me in the name of Jesus Christ."

I would have to do mental gymnastics and purposely take my mind off of the troublesome situation and put it on the cross, the open tomb, and a living Christ. When I would do this, my tears would dry and a certain peace would take up residence in my humming battlefield of a mind.

August came and went and I survived—barely.

September doesn't arrive in Florida like it does in

other parts of the world; it is just more of July and August—much more. But along with the rest of the nation's children, mine went off to school in September. Marvin left for the office when the kids left for school, and I was alone in that dreary house which refused to be cool. The heat, loneliness, and depression were wearying and staggering.

I had no desire to try to fix up the house or strength to look for another one. I didn't want to stay in Florida. Somehow all I could remember about Gadsden were the good times and the precious friends. I forgot that I had gotten so miserable there that I wanted to stop the world and get off.

The expense of moving to Florida was great, and I felt trapped by the fact that if we wanted to go home we couldn't afford it. Besides this, Marvin and I have both been responsible individuals and we had an obligation to meet.

Every day had a beige, desert sameness. At 6:00 A.M. I would get up and prepare a substantial breakfast with plenty of protein. We would have family devotions and prayers, and I would cheerfully kiss all the life in that house goodbye.

With Matthew's entrance into first grade, it was the first time in eighteen years that all my children were gone all day and it had a certain sadness to it. All those hours to myself were not nearly the ecstatic joy I had anticipated.

I would spend the hour from 7:00 to 8:00 watching the news, which is never very uplifting, whether the viewer is depressed or not. I would wash dishes (bemoaning my dishwasher in Alabama). I would make beds in rooms still crowded with cardboard boxes and trunks; there was no room for the contents anywhere. We had already rented a room in a "miniwarehouse."

With my morning work complete, I would go into the half-room that we called "the nook" to have my "quiet time." I had never had such a quiet "quiet time." I would listen to the Christian radio station, read my Bible, and try to pray.

After about an hour I would think hard, "What shall I do today? Whom shall I call? Where shall I go?"

The answers were always the same. "You will do nothing because you are stuck out in the country with cockroaches for company and there is nothing to do; you will call no one because there is no one to call; you will go nowhere because there is nowhere to go!" Boiling tears of frustration spilled profusely day after day, and I would beg God to make the clock move faster so my children would come home. I hunted for verses to use as weapons against the vicious assault on my mind.

One day at a meeting I was introduced to the "most vivacious and smiling" blond-haired woman of about thirty whose husband started and ran a Christian counseling center. When it was obvious we would enjoy each other, I asked her if she would be interested in becoming my prayer partner (something I had not done since my special friend and only real prayer partner "had split," as the kids say).

The very first day, I hit her with the biggie. I told her of my suicide attempt and asked her to pray with me about my depression. She immediately urged me to have a talk with one of the psychologists at the counseling center. I protested vigorously, saying I didn't want anyone in Tampa to know. I saw that as the only good thing about our move—I could keep the ugly secret to myself.

Somehow I didn't believe this girl with all her white teeth showing and light chatter could understand the depths to which I had plummeted. (About one year later this cheerful child of God slashed her wrists and very nearly died.)

Also, while I knew I was in trouble, I knew I was not insane. She was as amazed as I had been that it was not mandatory that I be under the care of a psychiatrist.

At her insistence, I set up an appointment with a very young, beautiful, size seven psychologist by the name of Ilene. I received abundant, concrete assistance almost immediately under the wise counsel of this brown-haired wonder who was not completely finished with her schooling. (That was why such a financially needy foundation had the aid of her talent.)

The providence of the Lord is full of wonderful surprises. While I was going weekly to be counseled by Ilene, I began to read *Hind's Feet On High Places* by Hannah Hurnard. Through that precious allegory, I began to change the wrong view I had of the Lord Jesus Christ. I began to see Him truly as the Kind Shepherd who was leading me and wanting to protect me so that He could lead me to the "high places," meaning more and more into Him and His purpose for my life. This book fit in with my Bible study where I read, "Be still, and know that I am God: I will be exalted among the heathen, I will be exalted in the earth" (Psalm 46:10, KJV).

As I backtracked in that Psalm, the words "know God, know God" rang in my spiritual ears.

Psalm 46 begins, "God is our refuge and strength, a very present help in trouble. Therefore will not we fear . . . God is in the midst of her; she shall not be moved: God shall help her, and that right early . . ." (KJV).

He very gently spoke to my heart, "I am the one who stuck you here in the country, where you once wanted to remain and watch the birds. You have changed, haven't you? I have given you this place to live because you said you would go anywhere with Me.

"I have stripped you of your friends and busyness for two reasons: one in answer to your prayer years earlier—'Conform me to the Lord Jesus, whatever the cost' — and secondly, because in your rush to serve Me you have never gotten to know Me. I want to have you learn to be with Me alone and to be comfortable in My presence, then you can go back to work for Me. You have a limited, distorted view of who I am and what I want to do with your life. So, Be still, and know that I am God."

The message was so clear and definite that I felt as if I had just enrolled in a college course called "Knowing God 101."

So, devoid of almost all outside people, I began to get to know God in all of His beauty and holiness.

This was not to take place in a large Bible class—no, just me and God alone. I was very uncomfortable at first. I was used to having my life filled with people, fun people, troubled people, but flesh and blood people.

I would squirm and fidget in my chair as my first grader must have been doing in his new chair. I would try to think of somewhere to go, someone to see. But my Schoolmaster said, *"Sit still* and *know."*

Little by little, line upon line, precept upon precept I learned, and I began to be comfortable.

My Teacher would say, "O taste and see that the Lord is good: blessed is the man that trusteth in him" (Ps. 34:8; KJV). He would show me the same verses that I had pointed out to literally hundreds of lost people. "I love you." "I am training you."

As I began to know and see God, I was, with the help of Ilene, beginning to see and know myself. I kept a chart on how I felt when things happened and what I did about those feelings.

I was amazed to add up a week's worth of real inner feelings about everything from fighting children to dirty clothes and see that the sum total of my feelings was anger. I had never considered myself an angry person.

As I peeled away the little angers at my children, my husband, and my circumstances, much like pulling leaves away from a head of cabbage, I saw at the core where my real anger was. I was shocked to find that I was venting this anger toward the same God I was learning about in the stillness of my little nook.

You can imagine my grief when I discovered that all my murmurings and bitterness were against this precious Shepherd who had laid down His life for me, who was promising me a rich and full life.

When the truth began to dawn on me that this hateful anger was getting in the way of everything, I began to make real progress toward getting well.

The first thing I had to do, in accordance with 1 John 1:9, was confess my anger as sin. The next thing I did was thank Him for bringing us to Florida and providing a house for us.

That day my fellowship was so restored with the Lord that I didn't notice the heat or the sand, and the house took on a real homey atmosphere as I bustled about baking cookies for the children. I was finally able to say, "Lord, if this is where you want me, I will stay here forever."

Along with this new-found comfort, the Lord impressed me with another lesson He would teach me—how to deal an effective blow to my enemy. Curiously, with all this growing knowledge and comfort about myself and the Lord, I was still being bombarded with, "It is just too hard; why not kill yourself and be done with the struggle? At least take a sleeping pill."

I would recognize that these suggestions were from the killer of Christians, and I would pray, "Lord, please make him leave me alone; help me!" But help would not come.

How could I have such peace and joy one moment and in the next moment be plagued with these taunts? I didn't know then how Satan had gained control through drugs. I looked for verses to use as the sharp Sword to thwart Satan's threats and growls, but for a long time I looked in vain.

Interspersed with little gleanings of truth and knowledge would come, "So, you are learning about the Kind Shepherd, are you? Where is He now, why doesn't He help you? It is all just a big nasty trick; you will see." On and on he would go, and again I became an unwilling partner as I listened to him.

One hopeless night late in November I lay in Marvin's arms sobbing, "Honey, I don't know what to do; all I can think about is dying. I have prayed for an accident, for cancer, for anything. I know it is wrong, but my mind is filled with death. I can't cope; I will never be able to."

He began to pray out loud, and I found some comfort in that and in the strong, brown arms that sheltered me. He brought as much comfort as any human could, but that was the trouble—he was only human.

The next morning my sameness overwhelmed me. I listened to the Christian radio station, read my Bible, and tried to pray. Satan came as sure as the hot sun began to rise in the east. He hurled his accusations at me and he slapped me hard with the same words, like pellets being thrown at a dying baby bird:

"Kill yourself—get out; kill yourself—get relief."

My Bible was open on my lap, and the tears were streaming down my cheeks onto the pages. I cried, "Dear Kind Shepherd, in the book I read you always came to help 'Much Afraid' when she would call, why don't You help me?"

I reached for a tissue to wipe my eyes and saw the pool forming on the page. I took the tissue to wipe off the shimmering, tiny pond. As I did, I read what was under the tear pool:

"The thief cometh not, but for to steal, and to kill, and to destroy: I am come that they might have life, and that they might have it more abundantly. I am the good shepherd: the good shepherd giveth his life for the sheep" (John 10:10,11; KJV).

My Savior said, "Honey, that's it—use it. Stick it into that old thief who has robbed and tried to kill and destroy you. Go ahead, use it now."

Momentarily, I questioned whether that simple verse, which I had quoted and read hundreds of times, packed the wallop needed to down my accuser. But the Guardian of my soul said it was.

I will repeat, almost verbatim, what I said because I have never forgotten nor will I ever forget the dramatic, emphatic, stunning victory that was won on the Mount Carmel of my mind that day: "Satan, these thoughts of suicide are not mine, I am not insane, they are not from God; THEY ARE YOURS! Jesus said, 'I am come that they might have life and that they might have it more abundantly.' Now I WANT TO LIVE, so in the NAME OF JESUS CHRIST, FLEE FROM ME."

I was shouting at Satan, and I almost looked around to see if anyone saw or heard me. I felt a little strange doing such a thing.

But all of a sudden I was whispering a tiny "thank you" to Jesus. I could feel His warm smile, much as a father who has just seen his son hit a home run. I had. I had hit a homer!

Immediately—yes, *immediately*—the oppressor was gone!

I could hardly believe the relief to my soul. My mind was calm, my heart was quiet and assured, and my whole being has never been more grateful than I was at that moment.

I could almost see him, that old serpent, slithering away, crippled. The Word of God had wounded him.

My quiet "thank you" was transformed into a loud "PRAISE THE LORD; JESUS CHRIST IS LORD; GREAT IS THE LORD AND GREATLY TO BE PRAISED."

The Lord reminded me of that verse that I had forgotten, "For God hath not given us the spirit of fear; but of power, and of love, and of a sound mind" (2 Tim. 1:7; KJV). Yes, the old spirit of fear himself was driven away, and God showed me the wonderful truth that He had given me the *power* and the *weapon* and a *sound mind.* Now I was really equipped for battle.

Victory was in my voice as I called the one who had stuck it out for better or worse, in sickness and health and for richer or poorer and I said, "Honey, it is all right, we can praise the Lord."

His relief came over the wires, and I knew for the first time what a cumbersome weight all of this had been for him.

Not long after this I was asked to give my testimony to a group of women who had no idea that I once had tried to commit suicide. I planned to give my regular (pre-1975) testimony and was praying about it as I scrubbed the kitchen floor on my hands and knees.

I was overwhelmed with the impression that I ought to tell the whole story. At first I said, "Oh no you don't, Satan. You can't trick me again. No one would understand that. They would think I am crazy." The verse came to me, "Let the redeemed of the Lord say so," and I knew God was telling me to obey Him. I just didn't know if I could do it.

The impulse was so strong by the time I got to the meeting I didn't know what to say. I had never, ever tried to put my experience into words. I still didn't really know all the reasons for my depression or how to express them.

After nervously picking at my lunch it was time to speak. I honestly told the ladies that I didn't know for sure what I was going to say, but they could help by answering two questions.

1. Are you ever weary of the battle of trying to live for Christ?

2. Do you ever consider throwing in the towel?

At first one or two shy hands slipped up.

Ashamed, I thought, "Uh huh, there is no need making a fool of myself; they would never understand."

All of a sudden, an attractive, slim, gray-haired lady pushed her chair noisily into the middle of the room, threw up her hand and said, "I am going to be honest—I have just about had it!" Her bravery forged the way, and hand after hand went up.

I said, "Let's pray as we have never prayed before." My prayer was not eloquent or flowery; there was no time for that. I was going to strip myself before these women, lay myself open, and I had no earthly idea how to word it.

The Lord instructed me, "Don't be afraid of their faces and don't worry about what you are going to say."

I continued, "Oh God, I have never been more dependent upon You. I don't see how You can get glory out of this, but here I am, just a size twelve dress covering a body—jump in and take over." And take over He did.

Faces were tear-stained and eyes red when I finished, and I don't even remember the words I said, but one after another the women came up and handed me their name tags with notes on the back. Their notes described the fierce battles they were going through and indicated their desire to know why these struggles were taking place and who was causing them and if God still cared about them.

Some wouldn't write their problem on the tag because they said it was too awful to record on paper; others shared heartaches that I didn't know existed.

That day I knew the Lord would never let me remain silent about what had transpired in my life. The Lord assured me He had comforted me not to make me comfortable but to make me a comforter. I could finally say, "Lord, it has all been worth it."

I wanted to write about what I was learning right then, but I knew I must wait and give sufficient time to prove to myself that the lessons were true and that the victory was lasting. I had won a particular battle over a particular issue with the appropriate use of God's Word. It was that simple. I would face many more battles with the serpent, but I had won that one.

Why did it take so long? I honestly don't know.

Why didn't God relieve me sooner? Again, I don't know. But if every agonizing moment of every dreary hour of every long day that I suffered made me one whit more sensitive and compassionate for a tormented humanity, and especially those of the household of faith, I say, "Thank God for every minute, and yes, *yes,* it was worth it."

That was three years ago and although our family has faced some of the most severe trials—financially, physically, and with our children—since then, Satan no longer has the freedom to tell me that the only answer for these times is a pill for escape or death. In fact, I have not had one suicidal thought since that moment of victory.

I have almost feared to record this because the victory was so dramatic and instantaneous, and I surely know that God deals differently with each of us. But I have come to grips with the fact that it is only because it *is* dramatic that I have something to write about—something that people will take notice of. It is so genuinely from God that I cannot be silent.

ELEVEN

No Longer a Weed

It was January 19, 1977. My palms were sweating and my heart was racing as I read aloud the last words of my first story written for my creative writing class.

My mouth was so dry, I could have started a fire in it. But these were not feelings of fear; they were feelings of delicious excitement as I looked around at the class of eighteen while the professor asked for comments.

Some offered genuinely kind criticism, which I needed. Some blankly said, "I like it," but couldn't say why. About three people, including the instructor, made some very good comments about my imagery and concrete descriptions, and when I walked out of class that day I couldn't stop smiling. I really felt good about myself.

As I bumbled down the hall and stairs with all the dewy-skinned young girls and the long-haired, bearded guys, I was thinking, "I am as good as anyone here; in fact, one day I might be great. Just look at them, not even dry behind the ears yet. I have all those years of experience behind me, and I'm just beginning to live."

How did I begin to have that positive self-image after nursing a super-negative one for years? Many factors are involved.

First of all, my family and friends have been so

supportive of me that I could hardly not get well. Equally important is that the Lord has replaced my simmering hostility with His love, joy, and peace, and has done it by His grace. Finally, part of the solution had to come from within myself if I was to ever feel good about me. It was hard for me to "love my neighbor as myself" when I didn't even like me. So I had to determine to stop knocking myself down and find some things I did like.

Even before the "Mount Carmel" victory I had begun to try to find some good things in me, to find what worth there was.

My first conscious effort was made one morning shortly after moving to Florida when it seemed Satan or one of his cohorts was sitting right beside me on the drainboard while I did dishes.

He wasn't very good company as he would jeer at me, "You aren't worth a plug nickel; too bad they found you. Why don't you try it again? They don't need you."

I reminded him of the little yellow note from my precious daughter that said she did need me. That helped me see that all children need their mother, even if she is ill.

Satan said, "She just said that; she didn't mean it. See how you grouched at them this morning. Shame, shame. This is a good day to do it; they won't be home for hours."

In this conversation I told him that if Marvin had to hire someone to clean, cook, and wash dishes, he would pay a minimum of ten dollars a day. So I started there. I hung on to the fact that I was worth ten dollars a day; it was a beginning.

As I won my major battle with the evil one, I began to gain more ground. I became worth more in my own eyes when I realized that I was worth the blood of God's own Son. The first time I trusted the Lord to teach a class through me and He did, I gained more ground. Little by little, I grappled with the dark part of me that seemed more comfortable with negativism and began to work on being positive. Even losing the ten pounds that I needed to lose helped me feel better about myself.

Then the Lord began to really encourage me about going to college for the first time to learn about writing.

I knew nothing about enrolling or registering for college. But as I began to gain self-confidence, I just got in my car and went to the campus one day. I was saying, "I can do anything I want to—the world is mine."

After being bawled out for not calling for an appointment to be counseled so I could have an appointment to be registered, I rushed home with my chin down, thinking, "I don't know anything about college; I can't do it. I will just stay home where it is safe."

But I reached way down into my self and grabbed the real me by the scruff of the neck and said, "Oh, no you don't, old girl. You have tried that and it's the pits. You get yourself back down there."

Finally, against all the rules, I bypassed two courses that were prerequisites to the creative writing course and got in.

The more I attended class, the more I saw how I had been deceived into believing that I was ignorant and would never do anything that amounted to much.

I began to believe that I was "fearfully and wonderfully made." I even got comfortable with my melancholy temperament and learned how to let the Spirit control the weaknesses such as depression and discouragement.

I started seeing my interest in literature and writing, in art and painting, as good traits.

God started asking me to express myself in those ways, and as I took the needed courses it seemed God placed me in just the perfect places to witness and counsel.

The very fact that I had been through depression and a suicide attempt made my witness more convincing. They couldn't say, "She doesn't live in the real world. She doesn't have the problems we do." Even with lost people, God had turned around something that could have destroyed my witness and strengthened it.

It was amazing to some that I would say, "No matter how hard it has been or will be, I want to be conformed to the image of Christ."

Several months ago a reporter came to interview me for a chapter in a book she and another author were doing about the "born-again phenomenon." She asked for about one hour of time.

She came at 4:00 P.M. and left at 9:00 P.M. Her notebook was crammed full and her mouth open after I candidly told her that becoming a Christian is free and very simple but living the Christian life can sometimes be costly and is never simple. I told her I had failed a lot, but that I was grateful for another chance.

Her final question was the impetus for this chapter: "What does the future hold for Marilee Horton?"

I surprised even my own pessimistic self by saying, with a genuine smile that I felt right down to the tip of my toes, "It is very bright. I am no longer a weed; God is making a flower out of me."

This stunned reporter became my friend that day, and it was with extreme joy that I introduced her to my Savior. About two months later she became my sister in the Lord as Jesus welcomed another lost sheep into the fold.

Her conversion helped me in so many ways. I saw that God's grace could still shine through my testimony; she trusted Christ and His Word in spite of my weakness. She didn't blame Jesus for my troubles but saw Him graciously meeting my needs.

Slogans like "something good is about to happen" used to aggravate me, but now I agree with such positive views of life. My heart is almost constantly filled with praise and joy that certainly has to be supernatural.

I still have some physical problems such as occasional migraines, but I have stopped condemning myself for having them; either God will remove them or He will say, "My grace is sufficient for you . . ." (2 Cor. 12:9).

Somehow, I don't even mind the headaches anymore. The pain is unpleasant, but inwardly I seem to almost rise above the pain and see God doing something good that I don't even know about yet. "Call to

Me, and I will answer you, and I will tell you great and mighty things, which you do not know" (Jer. 33:3). I believe trials for the purpose of purging and purifying are important, and I am grateful for them.

I was forty-one this year, and I want to send a telegram to the world and say, "Hey, I'm growing up at last, and guess what, I'm not a weed after all!"

Most importantly, I am mentally, emotionally, and spiritually healthy again. God is using me again, only this time not just to bring forth fruit, but *more fruit*. The next step is *much fruit*.

I truly believe God's Spirit is being released through me, and I see Him comforting people by using my life and witness as an example.

I am busier than ever, and that in itself is very therapeutic. I still love to keep house and cook, and I run from senior high to junior high to elementary school ballgames. I have fallen in love all over again with my husband. I still teach and train teachers. I lead two lovely women's Bible classes that have my heart beating right in them.

Life is vital, important, and as precious as it ever was before 1975, and even more so.

Recently we had a scare about a lump in my right neck lymph gland that had to be biopsied. I just hung on to the promise: "I shall not die but live and declare the works of the Lord" (Ps. 118:17). Part of the time I was mentally making funeral arrangements as I gave in to the old melancholy Marilee. But most of the time I had peace

I know that my time to die will come. When it does I will be carried to heaven by the angels—but that hour will not come until I am finished with my part in declaring the works of the Lord. Until then, I'm in no hurry.

As a preacher friend of ours says, "Sure I'm ready to go, but I'm going to hold on to the bedposts with all my might." It is normal to want to live, and I do so want to live.

My four children are into life "full-speed ahead," and I feel very good about them and their futures.

How do I feel about *my* circumstances? Content! I feel like I have been nursed by El Shaddai, the Strong One. I'm satisfied, full to overflowing with His Spirit, and happy.

I am even content to be in Florida. I miss the dear friends left behind, of course, but God has taught me things in the loneliness that I could not have learned while in the security of friends.

He has taught me I can make it now, because I do totally depend on Him, and that is what it takes. If it weren't for hours of solitude, I would never be able to write. Now He can trust me with the new friends who are very precious to me here.

It is my hope that, no matter what your circumstances are, you will thank God, confess your murmurings and ungratefulness, and claim the filling of the Holy Spirit.

Then trust Him by faith as you did for salvation and walk, moment by moment, in the Spirit.

It is my hope that this book has revealed the true source of all suicidal thoughts and plans and has offered some concrete help in using the only Weapon that is effective in putting the devil in his place.

The Word of God is vital. It is used by the Spirit to

draw us to Jesus. The Holy Spirit uses the Word to show us our sin, give us the faith to believe, and assure us that we have believed.

The Word feeds us when we are hungry. It quenches our thirst as nothing else can.

The Word is our comfort in despair and our word of consolation to a troubled world.

But most of all the Word is vital for living these last days when the battle is going to be roughest, because Satan sees his impending doom and he will unleash all the demons of hell to oppress the children of God.

God says we are "more than conquerors through him that loved us" (Rom. 8:37, KJV). So, shore up your fronts with the Word; fill in the holes in your armor. Sharpen your Sword, then *resist the devil* and he will flee from you.

Declare the works of the Lord!